DEFENDING JESUS' CRUCIFIXION

against Islamic Revision of Christian History

REMINISCENT OF THE rationalist apologetical approach to Muslims pioneered by Carl Gottlieb Pfander, Herbert focuses with laser-like intensity on the Qur'an's claim that Jesus Christ was not crucified. He begins with an overview of the historical record and theological necessity of Christ's crucifixion, then juxtaposes six centuries of universally agreed testimony against the Qur'an's seventh-century assertion to the opposite. Gently, but systematically, Herbert proceeds to deconstruct the revisionist historical accounts of such well-known Muslim writers as 'Abd al-Jabbār and Muhammad 'Ata ur-Rahim, before turning his attention to the spurious *Gospel of Barnabas*. An appropriate gift for your seeking, questioning Muslim friend.

Peter Pikkert, Ph.D
Co-author, *A Comparative Dictionary of Religious Terms in Islam and Christianity (2020)*

THE RESURRECTION OF Jesus is the very foundation and heart of Christianity. If Jesus did not rise from the dead, Christianity is the greatest hoax in all of history. The biblical gospel rests on the death, burial and resurrection of Jesus. One certain fact acknowledged by the vast majority of scholars is the death of Jesus on a Roman cross. Islam has rejected this historical fact based on 40 vague Arabic words in the Qur'an, Sura 4:157, written six centuries after the death and resurrection of Jesus. In denying the death of Jesus, Islam has also rejected the resurrection, thus undercutting the gospel message—and this to the peril of the souls of Muslims all around the world.

In this book, David Herbert addresses these important points in canvasing all the evidence regarding the crucifixion and death of Jesus. Through an analysis of the New Testament, the early church fathers, the creeds of the church and extra-biblical sources from Jewish and Greco-Roman authors, Herbert presents a formidable case for the historicity of the crucifixion and death of Jesus. I would recommend Herbert's book to anyone who has an elementary knowledge of Islam. After reading this book, the reader will quickly learn how foreign and different the Jesus of Islam is from the historic Jesus of the Bible.

Tony Costa, Ph.D.
Professor of Islam and Apologetics, Toronto Baptist Seminary, Canada

WHEN DEFENDING the gospel of Jesus Christ, Christians have a tendency to zero in on the *resurrection*, because they believe it is the most important doctrine to support and defend: if Jesus didn't rise from the dead, then we are all damned. Yet the resurrection is not a concern for Muslims at all, due to one verse in the Qur'an, Sura 4:157, which says Jesus *never died* on the cross. If he never died, then it stands to reason there was no resurrection, and the fact that about 500 saw him following the crucifixion is no surprise. Therefore, when engaging Muslims, Christians need to focus instead on Jesus' *crucifixion*, which is precisely what David Herbert does in this book.

Herbert's entire emphasis is rather unique. Rather than just argue for the crucifixion *theologically*, as most of us would tend to do, he looks at this event *historically*, pointing to a myriad of early historical figures both pagan and Christian, who support Jesus' crucifixion in the centuries following it. These he compares with the much later Muslim sources, presenting a solid contrasting view between them.

He then moves on to two major and influential Muslim documents, a fourteenth-century forgery, *Gospel of Barnabas*, and a very recent popular book, *Jesus: Prophet of Islam*. Both of these documents confront, among other things, Christ's crucifixion. Herbert, by using historical documentation as support, proves just how ahistorical and ill-conceived both of these popular Muslim writings are.

It is here that Herbert's book, in my opinion, proves its true mettle. The crucifixion of Jesus is so well attested historically that this small verse in Chapter 4 of the Qur'an that categorically denies it creates an enormous dilemma for Muslim apologists, whose only recourse is to fall back on such erroneous and historically inept forgeries as the *Gospel of Barnabas*. Thanks to Herbert, we have an easy-to-read, yet well argued response to both of these popular Muslim works.

Because the crucifixion has to be at the centre of our engagement with Muslims, I would encourage anyone interested in engaging with them to read this book, and employ Herbert's well-thought-out arguments. This is one book that should be in the library of anyone who seeks to defend our Lord Jesus Christ among our Muslim friends.

Jay Smith, Ph.D.
Apologist and polemicist, UK

AS A CROSS-CULTURAL worker in the UK, this book has reminded me of the historical evidence we have for the crucifixion, as well as providing me with a better understanding of the Islamic doctrine and its roots. Herbert enables us to approach this key event through the lens of historical integrity, helping us build upon our confidence in Christ's death and resurrection found in Scripture by thoroughly presenting and evaluating the historical evidence. He graciously, yet clearly, deconstructs the Islamic interpretation of the crucifixion, equipping us, as workers, to defend our beliefs confidently, while challenging our friends. This book is a must-read for those seeking to share the gospel with Muslims.

Jessica Brie
Cross-cultural worker, Pioneers, UK

DEFENDING JESUS' CRUCIFIXION

against Islamic Revision of Christian History

DAVID HERBERT

www.joshuapress.com | hesedandemet.com

H&E Publishing, Peterborough, Ontario, Canada

Cover and book design by Janice Van Eck

ISBN 978-1-989174-42-5

Patti Halliday B.Sc.N.

*For thirteen years (2005–2018) Patti, as a faithful team member,
interviewed individuals for five questionnaires. The compiled responses
were used in the books that I have written. Her greatest joy,
as opportunities arose, was sharing
the gospel of Jesus Christ.*

Contents

Foreword

In the hymn "For the Mahometans," penned by the hymnwriting genius Charles Wesley in the eighteenth century, there is the following couplet:

> O might the blood of sprinkling cry
>> For those who spurn the sprinkled blood!

Wesley was praying that despite the fact that Muslims reject the crucifixion of Christ—and thus his propitiatory and atoning work—"the blood of sprinkling" might prove efficacious and save some of them. The prominence of Islam's denial of the crucifixion is such that any discussion of or prayer for Muslims had to include mention of this element of historical revisionism. Now, in this excellent summative work, David Herbert tackles this central difference between Christianity and Islam, though obviously with much more detail.

Herbert first examines the nature and reality of crucifixion in the Roman *imperium*, and then the overwhelming New Testament witness to the historical veracity of the cross of Christ. Pagan and Christian sources from the ancient world are then discussed, all of which indubitably point to the remarkable reality that Jesus, whom Islam honours as a sinless prophet, died an ignominious death at the hands of Roman state authorities. As Herbert cites the agnostic scholar Bart Ehrman, given the horror, disgust and shame associated with the cross in the Græco-Roman world, no one in their right mind would have declared that a man who died in this manner was the Saviour of the world!

The centrality of the cross is also found in the Niceno-Constantinopolitan Creed—usually known as the Nicene Creed—which Herbert looks at in some detail since it confesses that Jesus "was crucified for us under Pontius Pilate." The importance of this confession is given further weight by the fact that in this Christian creed we have this historical figure mentioned—namely, Pontius Pilate, who was anything but a follower of the Messiah! He is there in the creed because at the heart of the Christian faith is the *historicity* of the crucifixion of Jesus at the command of Pilate.

Dr. Herbert does not overlook the way in which Islam has used the bogus *Gospel of Barnabas* to buttress its claim that Jesus did not die on the cross. He rightly shows that this late-medieval forgery has no historical value when it comes to reporting on events of the first century.

Herbert concludes with two chapters in which he engages in a critical, though loving, discussion of Islamic theological reflection on the cross. He demonstrates without a shadow of a doubt that Islamic theology must founder on its denial of the historicity of the cross.

In summary, this is an excellent study that I hope receives a wide readership, especially among Muslims. May it be a powerful means in the hands of the triune God in answering Charles Wesley's eighteenth-century prayer: "O might the blood of sprinkling cry / For those who spurn the sprinkled blood!"

Michael A.G. Haykin, FRHistS
Professor of Church History
The Southern Baptist Theological Seminary
Louisville, Kentucky

Acknowledgements

MY INTEREST IN investigating how Christianity and Islam differ in their understanding of Jesus' crucifixion can be attributed to my son Trent. While living near the London Mosque, he began to distribute a tract informing the Islamic community of the person of Jesus Christ from a Christian perspective.

I joined him in this endeavour, and through my interaction with Muslims, I became aware that they did not believe Jesus was crucified but rather that another took his place. Shortly after I began the research for this book, I formulated a questionnaire.

Over the next two-and-a-half years, 700 people were interviewed. To Patti Halliday, Leah Postma, Matthew Arnold, David Cline and his son, Jacob, Calvin Foster and his son, Noah, and Trent Herbert, I am deeply indebted for the hours they spent getting the questionnaires completed.

I appreciate the Muslim scholars, both nationally and internationally, who took time to read the manuscript.

The Christian community also played a significant role. My son Trent and my wife Irene should receive honourable mention as they read the manuscript a number of times. I would commend two fellow historians: Andrew McLeod, B.A., M.Div., for his editorial work and Michael Haykin, Ph.D., for reading the manuscript and writing the foreword.

For Christian scholars outside of Canada, I want to express my appreciation: A.H. Mathias Zahniser, Ph.D. (Greenville College scholar in residence, Greenville, Illinois) and Ayman Ibrahim, Ph.D. (The Southern Baptist Theological Seminary, Louisville, Kentucky). Lastly, I want to thank John Gilchrist, a South African lawyer and Christian and Islamic apologist, who sent me his unpublished manuscript, *The Qur'an and the Historical Jesus*.

Introduction

CRUCIFIXION (*crux*), BURNING (*crematio*) or decapitation (*decollatio*)
were known as the most brutal forms of execution in the ancient
world. Without a doubt, crucifixion ranked first. "Originating in
Mesopotamia and Persia, crucifixion was perfected by the Romans,
who saw it as the most shameful mode of death."[1]

Is it any wonder that Cicero (106–43 B.C.), one of Rome's most
famous lawyers and orators, when commenting concerning the
unimaginable cruelty of crucifixion, wrote:

> … and the very word "cross," should be far removed not only
> from a Roman citizen but even from his thoughts, his eyes,
> and his ears.[2]

Cicero made this statement in 63 B.C. when he was defending Gaius
Rabirius who was being tried for high treason (*perduellio*). If convict-
ed, the aged senator would have been crucified on the Campus
Martius. The consequences for such a punishment were indeed

---

1 François Pieter Retief and Louise Cilliers, "The history and pathology of crucifixion," *South African Medical Journal* 93 (2003): 938.

2 Cicero, *Pro Rabirio*, trans. H. Grose Hodge in *Loeb Classical Library* (Cambridge:
Harvard University Press, 1952), 5:16.

dire. Crucifixion "would have symbolically deprived Rabirius of his Roman citizenship, and status as a freeman, disgracing him and his family for generations."[3]

Noted Roman historian, Cornelius Tacitus (*ca.* A.D. 56–120), recorded that Nero (A.D. 37–68) charged the Christians with setting Rome ablaze for six days in A.D. 64. Since the early believers in Christ were not protected by Roman citizenship, this maniacal emperor inflicted despicable tortures upon them.

They were wrapped in the skins of wild animals and perished by being torn to pieces by dogs; or *they were nailed to crosses* and, when daylight had gone, burned to provide lighting at night.[4]

Nero
(A.D. 37–68)

Crucifixion, a highly effective punishment, was available to the Roman Senate and the provincial governors if they felt that Roman authority was being jeopardized in any way. Typically, it was reserved "for slaves, brigands, and rebels and occasionally enemy generals."[5]

For example, Josephus (A.D. 37–100), a Jewish historian, recorded what happened to nearly 500 desperate men and women who daily crept outside of the walls of Jerusalem, their besieged city, in search of food during the closing months of the Jewish revolt in A.D. 66–70. The Roman commander, Titus

---

3   *Brill's Companion to Cicero: Oratory and Rhetoric*, ed. James M. May (Leiden: Brill, 2002), 130. Rabirius was later set free. See Messalla, "Political trials in Ancient Rome: the curious case of Gaius Rabirius," *Corvinus* (April 21, 2017); http://corvinusnl/2017/04/21/political-trials-in-ancient-rome-the-curious-case-of-gaius-rabirius/ (accessed December 30, 2017) for the details of his peculiar acquittal.

4   Tacitus, *Annales* 15:44 in David W. Chapman and Eckhard J. Schnabel, *The Trial and Crucifixion of Jesus: Texts and Commentary* (Tübingen: Mohr Siebeck, 2015), 193. Italics not in the original.

5   Chapman and Schnabel, *Trial and Crucifixion of Jesus*, 532.

(A.D. 39–81), not having sufficient soldiers to guard these starving inhabitants, handed them over to be crucified.

> [Titus] hoped [those in the city] might quickly surrender in response to the sight, lest they be handed over, suffering the same fate. The soldiers, on account of anger and hatred, for a joke nailed in various forms those who had been captured; and because of the multitude, *both the space lacking for the crosses and crosses were lacking for bodies.*[6]

The purpose of the book

To the modern mind, the idea of crucifixion is undoubtedly linked to the life of Jesus Christ. Both Christianity and Islam, consisting of 4.1 billion adherents worldwide,[7] make reference to it in their sacred texts—the Bible and the Qur'an. But each has a radically different understanding of this historical event. The author's goal is to examine the historical sources relating to Jesus' crucifixion from A.D. 33[8] until A.D. 381 in order to determine whether the Christian understanding or the Islamic one is correct.

The Christian perspective—Jesus crucified

A historical discussion of the impact of Jesus' crucifixion from the first century to the Niceno-Constantinopolitan Creed of 381 must begin by examining how the New Testament was influenced by the Old Testament. The biblical foundation—both historically and theologically—concerning the death of Jesus on a cross can only be established when one sees how these two testaments work together.

Four non-biblical sources, most importantly, Josephus and Tacitus, moved the investigation outside the Christian realm. Their

---

6 Josephus, *The Jewish War* 5.450–451 in Chapman and Schnabel, *Trial and Crucifixion of Jesus*, 651. Italics not in the original.

7 Pew Reseach Center, "Christians remain world's largest religious group, but they are declining in Europe," (April 5, 2017); http://www.pewresearch.org/fact-tank/2017/04/05/christians-remain-worlds-largest-religious-group-but-they-are-declining-in-europe/ (accessed December 30, 2017).

8 See Harold W. Hoehner, "Chronology" in Joel B. Green, Scot McKnight and I. Howard Marshall, eds., *Dictionary of Jesus and the Gospels: A Compendium of Contemporary Biblical Scholarship* (Downers Grove: IVP Academic, 1992), 118–122, in which he gives an excellent defense, both historically and scientifically, for the date A.D. 33 as opposed to A.D. 30.

record of Jesus' crucifixion greatly increased the historical validity of the New Testament account. Upon this New Testament foundation, the testimony of four early church fathers as primary sources will be considered, namely: Ignatius of Antioch (*ca.* A.D. 35–110), Justin Martyr (A.D. 100–165), Irenaeus (*ca.* A.D. 130–202) and Lactantius (*ca.* A.D. 250–325).

The rise of Emperor Constantine (A.D. 272–337), during the fourth century, caused Christianity's role to change dramatically. With the Edict of Milan in A.D. 313, Constantine granted the illicit religion of Christianity equal status with other religions within the Roman empire. This new religious freedom provided a basis for the creation of the creeds of Nicaea (A.D. 325) and Constantinople (A.D. 381)—both creeds accepted Jesus' crucifixion and death as a historical fact.

A historical thread—Pontius Pilate

> … Pontius Pilate, the most complex of biblical characters. The subject of countless biographies, stage plays, films and documentaries, the inspiration for poetry, literature, drama, music, and opera, he still remains an enigmatic figure.[9]

Even though Colum Hourihane's book traces the artistic characterization of Pilate from the early Christian writings up to the fifteenth century, his claim, found in the "Introduction," is totally appropriate for today. By doing a search for "Pontius Pilate" on the American Theological Library Association (ATLA) database, one can find thirty-seven entries consisting of books and theological articles from 2000 to 2019.[10]

Thus, it would seem fitting for Pontius Pilate to be the historical thread from A.D. 33 to 381. Without his association with Jesus' crucifixion, he would be as unknown as the two Roman prefects, Coponius and Valerius Gratus, whose governorships preceded his.

---

9 Colum Hourihane, *Pontius Pilate, Anti-Semitism and the Passion in Medieval Art* (Princeton: Princeton University Press, 2009), 1.

10 See "Pontius Pilate," via AtlaSerials (accessed November 29, 2019).

Prior to 1961—outside of a few coins and only eight written sources, one by Philo of Alexandria (*ca.* 25 B.C.–*ca.* A.D. 50),[11] six by Josephus[12] and the New Testament record—there was no archaeological evidence of Pilate's existence. Such limited documentation caused some historians to question whether he was indeed a real person.

However, Italian archaeologists ended such speculation in June 1961. At Caesarea Maritima by the Mediterranean Sea, the site of Pilate's administrative capital and military headquarters, they found a limestone marker.[13] It bore this inscription (the bracketed sections have been added):

DI]S TIBERIUM
...PO]NTIUS PILATUS
...PRAEF]ECTUS IVDA[EA]E
[FECIT D]E[DICAVIT]

A literal translation would be:

To the honorable gods (this) Tiberium
Pontius Pilate,
Prefect of Judea,
had dedicated[14]

In 2017, R. Steven Notley made this salient observation:

As we have seen, archaeology increases our understanding of the complex figure of Pontius Pilate. Nothing in the physical

---

11 Philo, *De legatione ad Gaium* (*On the Embassy to Gaius*) 299–305, in Chapman and Schnabel, *Trial and Crucifixion of Jesus*, 167–174.

12 The six references are found in Chapman and Schnabel, *Trial and Crucifixion of Jesus*, 175–192: Josephus, *Bellum judaicum* (*The Jewish War*) 2.169–174; 2:175–177; *Antiquitates judaicae* (*Jewish Antiquities*) 18.55–59; 18.60–62; 18.63–64; 18.85–89.

13 Anne Rowe, "Historical Notes: Pontius Pilate: a name set in stone," *Independent* (April 2, 1999); http://www.independent.co.uk/news/people/historical-notes-pontius-pilate-a-name-set-in-stone-1084786.html (accessed June 27, 2016).

14 "Biblical Archaeology 40: The Pilate Stone" (September 20, 2011); https://theosophical.wordpress.com/2011/09/20/biblical-archaeology-40-the-pilate-stone/ (accessed July 5, 2016).

settings of the historical accounts is inconsistent with the result of the past 60 years—just the opposite.[15]

Since Pilate's existence has now been firmly established archaeologically, it adds greater credence to the historicity of Jesus' existence and, more importantly, his death on the cross.

The Islamic perspective—Jesus was *not* crucified

In the Qur'an, Jesus is viewed as one of the five elite prophets.[16] He was mortal but not divine. Since he is considered to be righteous,[17] it would have been the gravest of all travesties to subject a person of Jesus' esteem to such an ignominious death on the cross. "God would never have let Jesus be killed by his enemies—especially not by the shame-laden means of crucifixion."[18]

Thus, the Qur'an makes this one and only statement denying Jesus' crucifixion:[19]

And for their sayings, "Surely we killed the Messiah, Jesus, son of Mary, the messenger of God"—*yet they did not kill him, nor did they crucify him,* but it (only) seemed like (that) to them. Surely those who differ about him are indeed in doubt about him. They have no knowledge about him, only the following conjecture. *Certainly, they did not kill him.* No! God raised him up to Himself. God is mighty, wise.[20]

Muslims have no difficulty in believing that there was a crucifixion at the end of Jesus' earthly ministry. But an overwhelming majority strenuously deny that *Jesus* was the one who was crucified. By accepting

---

15 R. Steven Notley, "Pontius Pilate: Sadist or Saint?" *Biblical Archaeology Review* 23 (July/August, 2017): 59.

16 The five elite prophets are Noah, Abraham, Moses, Jesus and Muhammad. Some include Adam as the sixth.

17 Sura 3:46. "He will speak to the people (while he is still) in the cradle and in adulthood, and (he will be) one of the righteous." All Qur'anic quotations will be from *The Qur'an: A New Annotated Translation*, trans. A.J. Droge (Bristol: Equinox), 2013.

18 A.H. Mathias Zahniser, *The Mission and Death of Jesus in Islam and Christianity* (Maryknoll: Orbis, 2008), 234.

19 Some Muslim scholars also include Sura 3:55.

20 Sura 4:157–158. Italics added.

this position, Muslims, most definitely those who are academics, must interpret the historical events after A.D. 33 in light of this theological stance.

Two prominent Muslim polemicists, one from the tenth century and the other from the twentieth century, have attempted to present a historical interpretation from A.D. 33 to 381 to deny Jesus' death on the cross. The former is 'Abd al-Jabbār (A.D. 930–1025) and the latter, Muhammad 'Ata ur-Rahim (d. 1978).

Born in Iran, 'Abd al-Jabbār "rose to great heights as an author, theologian and jurist."[21] He authored *The Critique of Christian Origins* (A.D. 995), one of the earliest Islamic interpretations of the first four centuries of Christian history. Throughout his book, 'Abd al-Jabbār deconstructed Christianity "with a lengthy critique of Christian doctrine, scripture, history and practice."[22] As a defender of Islam, 'Abd al-Jabbār gave an explanation why he believed Christianity became perverted.

> If you scrutinize the matter, you will find that the Christians became Romans and fell back to the religions of the Romans. You will not find that the Romans became Christians.[23]

Muhammad 'Ata ur-Rahim, a year before his death, published *Jesus: Prophet of Islam*.[24] The introduction to the first edition clearly depicted the tone of the book,

> From this work, it is clear that there is no longer any such thing as the Christian religion. Christianity is over. The myth has finally exploded.
>
> Why this work is so welcome is that, first of all, it looks at the roots of the Christian phenomenon from the only point of view from which it can be properly understood—I mean, the Muslim

---

21 Gabriel Said Reynolds, "The Rise and Fall of Qādi 'Abd al-Jabbār," *International Journal of Middle East Studies* 37 (2005): 4.

22 Gabriel Said Reynolds, *A Muslim Theologian in the Sectarian Milieu: 'Abd al-Jabbār and the Critique of Christian Origins* (Leiden: Brill, 2004), 2.

23 'Abd al-Jabbār, *The Critique of Christian Origins: Qādī 'Abd al-Jabbār's (d. 415/1025) Islamic Essay on Christianity*, trans. and ed. Gabriel Said Reynolds and Samir Khalili Samir (Provo: Brigham Young University Press, 2010), 103.

24 Muhammad 'Ata ur-Rahim, *Jesus: Prophet of Islam* (Norfolk: Diwan Press, 1977).

point of view. It is the sole vantage point from which it can be surveyed, because *Islam is the inheritor of Jesus.*[25]

A former lieutenant colonel in the Indian army, Rahim maintained that the Muslim belief in a one-God unity, more commonly called Unitarianism, flourished from the New Testament period of the first century A.D. to the twentieth century. Joseph Priestley

Joseph Priestley
(1733-1804)

(1733–1804), a renowned chemist and the one who was credited with the discovery of oxygen, was highlighted. To demonstrate the importance of Priestley, the founder of modern Unitarianism, Rahim directly quoted twelve pages from two of Priestley's books, *The History of Jesus* (1786) and *A History of the Corruptions of Christianity* (1797).[26]

Oddbjørn Leirvik from Oslo, Norway, made this astute observation concerning Rahim's book, *Jesus: Prophet of Islam*: "Despite the title, his book is more a study of Christianity than a book about Jesus."[27]

Ahmad Thomson (1950–), a British lawyer and convert to Islam in 1966,[28] was a very close friend of Colonel Rahim. In 1996, he took it upon himself to revise, reformat and update *Jesus: Prophet of Islam*. Even though the book had been written some two decades previously, Thomson did not alter its main thesis.

Questionnaire

Since January 2005, five questionnaires have been used to add an important human dimension to the research for all my books. The present one concerning Christianity and Islam was the first where

---

25 Muhammad 'Ata ur-Rahim and Ahmad Thomson, *Jesus: Prophet of Islam*, rev. ed. (London: Ta-Ha Publishers, 1996), xi–xii. Italics not in the original text.

26 Rahim, *Jesus, Prophet of Islam*, 170–182.

27 Oddbjørn Leirvik, *Images of Jesus Christ in Islam*, 2nd ed. (New York: Continuum, 2010), 154.

28 He was born in Northern Rhodesia, today Zambia, as Martin Thomson.

the interviewers approached individuals at their homes.

The thesis of the questionnaire, composed of five questions, read as follows:

> To examine the historical sources in order to judge the validity of the claims made by Christianity and Islam concerning Jesus' death on the cross.[29]

In conducting the questionnaire, the interviewers went to three locations in London, Ontario, Canada. The first was outside the gates of the University of Western Ontario (UWO). The second was Victoria Park located in central London—the quiet and casual setting was conducive to interacting with people. Lastly, they went door-to-door in south-east London.

Even though the topic, related to Christianity and Islam, was undoubtedly contemporary and somewhat controversial, the majority of people were receptive and pleased to assist. A few declined to participate; it was difficult to ascertain whether they felt uncomfortable discussing religious issues or the mere mention of Islam caused some uneasiness.

Personal convictions and truth

"You cannot write this book from an unbiased Christian viewpoint," a business student challenged me after completing the questionnaire.[30] I immediately responded by reminding him that he, as a Muslim, would have the same difficulty if he were the author. This exchange took place on the sidewalk outside UWO.

Throughout the three decades that I have been writing books, it has been my policy to identify myself as an evangelical Christian. A reviewer of my book, *Charles Darwin's Religious Views* (2009), made this response concerning my personal conviction,

> As a biography of Charles Darwin's (1809 to 1882) life, this slim book is one of the best I have ever read. It is scholarly yet quite readable....

---

29 See Appendix for the questionnaire titled, "Jesus' Death on the Cross—Christian or Muslim Views" to find the responses and the results.

30 Interview #158 (October 1, 2015).

In the book's preface the author states, "Although I am presenting my research on Charles Darwin's Christianity, my own religious perspective will be continually before the reader. Consequently, I believe that it is very important for me to declare my particular bias."

When I read this, I thought to myself, "Oh No! Herbert (the author) is going to ask the reader to accept the supernatural and attempt to change the facts, in this case, with respect to Darwin's life." (I've evaluated other books on science and religion or science versus religion and these two things seem to always occur.) … Therefore, when the author says he is going to "declare [his] particular [religious] bias," I found that this bias was not obvious and very subtle (at least to me). Yes, he tells us he is a true believer in a Creator (and other things like this) but he does not let this bias interfere with the true facts regarding the story of Darwin. As well, any bias the author did present was not convincing (again, at least to me).[31]

I so much appreciated Steve Pletko's commendation. My personal commitment did not deter me from discovering what Charles Darwin believed. By using his writings, especially his voluminous letters, I was able to determine the essence of his religious views.

Muslim scholar Mehnaz Afridi, director of Holocaust, Genocide and Interfaith Education at Manhattan College, New York, authored *Shoah through Muslim Eyes*.[32] Afridi successfully demonstrated that the Holocaust is a historical fact. Despite opposition from both Muslim and Jewish sectors, she arrived at this conclusion through the use of primary sources—namely, by interviewing Holocaust survivors and by visiting the Dachau concentration camp.

Similarly, *Avenue of Spies* by Alex Kershaw described the courageous exploits of an American medical doctor, Sumner Jackson, his wife and son, Philip, who joined the French resistance against Nazism. All three experienced the horrors of German concentration

---

31 For the complete review, see Steve Pletko, "An Important Study of Charles Darwin, one of the most significant figures of our time" (June 26, 2009); https://www.amazon.com/Charles-Darwins-religious-views-evolutionist/dp/1894400305 (accessed July 5, 2016).

32 Mehnaz M. Afridi, *Shoah through Muslim Eyes* (Cambridge: Academic Studies Press, 2017).

camps. In his "Acknowledgments," Kershaw noted that Philip, now in his eighties, willingly "endured hours of interviews over the phone and in person in Paris over several years."[33] His daughter, Loraine Riemer, provided crucial family letters and other primary sources.

The use of primary sources will similarly characterize this book. Through an examination of the New Testament, the writings of non-Christian historians and Christian authors from the first four centuries A.D., the truth will emerge that Jesus Christ *was* crucified and died. No middle ground solution will be countenanced. The Islamic position that Jesus was *not* crucified and another took his place[34] or he escaped death by other means will be shown to lack historical support and veracity.

---

33 Alex Kershaw, *Avenue of Spies: A True Story of Terror, Espionage, and One American's Family's Heroic Resistance in Nazi-occupied Paris* (New York: Broadway, 2015), 229.

34 The Qur'an does not mention that someone acted as Jesus' substitute. Islamic tradition, however, specifies that it was Judas, a disciple of Jesus. See "Judas Crucified in Jesus' Place" in Zahniser, *The Mission and Death of Jesus in Islam and Christianity*, 79–94.

CHAPTER 1

A scriptural defence of Jesus' crucifixion

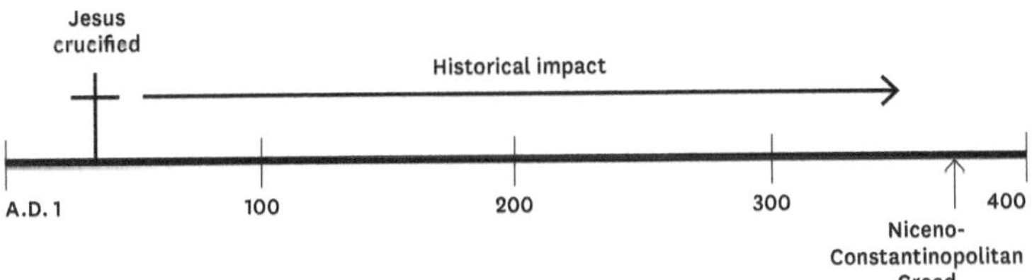

Jesus Christ in the Old Testament

DURING ONE OF Jesus' post-resurrection encounters with his disciples, he made a statement that would forever alter the interpretation of the Old Testament:

> Then beginning with Moses and with all the prophets, He explained to them the things concerning Himself in all the Scriptures.[1]

In the prologue of his Gospel, John identified Jesus Christ as God and also the Creator. He stated: "All things came into being through

---

1   Luke 24:27. To complete the three-fold sections of the Old Testament, Jesus refers to the Psalms in Luke 24:44.

Him, and apart from Him nothing came into being that has come into being."[2] Thus, the Creator-God of Genesis 1:1—the first book of Moses—was none other than Jesus himself.

The apostle Paul continued the same theme. To substantiate Jesus Christ's role as Creator, he inserted a hymn that was sung by the early church:

> He is the image of the invisible God, the firstborn [*prōtotokos*] of all creation. For by Him all things were created, *both* in the heavens and on earth, visible and invisible.[3]

The hymn continues:

> For it was the *Father's* good pleasure for all the fullness to dwell in Him, and through Him to reconcile all things to Himself, having made peace through the blood of His cross.[4]

The book of Isaiah provides two important prophecies as it relates to Jesus being the reconciler of all things through his death on the cross. First, Isaiah 40 announces that God would send a forerunner to announce the arrival of the Messiah. All three Synoptic Gospels,[5] quoting Isaiah, identify this forerunner as John the Baptist.

Mark's Gospel states:

> As it is written in Isaiah the prophet:
> "Behold, I send My messenger ahead of You
> Who will prepare Your way."[6]

Second, in one of the most revered chapters in the Old Testament, namely Isaiah 53, the beloved prophet revealed the horrific ordeal that the Suffering Servant would endure when he wrote:

———————————

2   John 1:3

3   Colossians 1:15–16. Paul reinforced the concept that Jesus was Creator by choosing the word *prōtotokos*, meaning preeminent. Italics in the original.

4   Colossians 1:19–20. Italics in the original.

5   Matthew 3:1–6; Mark 1:2–6; Luke 3:3–6. The word synoptic is derived from the Greek words *sun* (together) and *opsis* (view)—a seeing together.

6   Mark 1:2.

Surely our griefs He Himself bore,
And our sorrows He carried;
Yet we ourselves esteemed Him stricken,
Smitten of God, and afflicted.
But He was pierced through for our transgressions,
He was crushed for our iniquities;
The chastening for our well-being *fell* upon Him,
And by His scourging we are healed.[7]

The apostle Peter had no doubt that the one prophesied in Isaiah 53 was Jesus. Referencing this passage, Peter wrote about Jesus' sacrificial death in these terms:

and He Himself bore our sins in His body on the cross, so that we might die to sin and live to righteousness; for by His wounds you were healed.[8]

All the New Testament authors were steeped in the teachings of the Old Testament. Included also would be Luke, a Gentile, who wrote the Gospel that bears his name and the book of Acts. His close association with the apostles reveals that he too truly understood the importance of the Law of Moses, the Prophets and the Psalms.[9]

Committed to Jesus as their personal Lord and Redeemer, these men used every possible opportunity to draw upon the teachings of the Old Testament—God's divine revelation. They were convinced of this truth: the Jesus of the New Testament was indeed the same of whom the Old prophesied, thus joining these two Testaments together.

Immanuel—God with us

"Behold, the virgin shall be with child and shall bear a Son, and they shall call His name Immanuel," which translated means, "God with us."[10]

---

7   Isaiah 53:4–5. Italics in the original.
8   1 Peter 2:24.
9   Luke 24:44.
10 Matthew 1:23.

Matthew took this remarkable announcement to establish two major theological themes concerning Jesus' supernatural conception as foreshadowed in Isaiah 7:14: his virgin birth and his name Immanuel. No other author of the New Testament, with the exception of Matthew, used this title of Jesus. Immanuel was a transliteration from the Hebrew, meaning "God with us." "Matthew's primary doctrinal intent was, of course, Christological. Conceived of a virgin, Jesus was a messianic king but also the embodiment of divine presence among his people."[11]

A parallel verse, referring to God being among his people, is found in John's Gospel: "And the Word [Jesus Christ] became flesh, and dwelt among us, and we saw His glory."[12] The word "dwelt" in Greek is *eskēnōsen*,[13] which could be rendered "tabernacled." It was reminiscent of the tabernacle in the Old Testament, where God met with his people of Israel. Now, in the person of Jesus, God was "tabernacling" among his people.

The purpose of Jesus' coming into the world was that "He will save His people from their sins."[14] After Adam's and Eve's rebellion, God promised that a Messiah, or Deliverer, would restore the righteousness that was lost in the Garden of Eden. "But when the fullness of the time came, God sent forth His Son, born of a woman, born under the Law"[15] so that he might redeem a fallen humanity and then adopt them into his family. This was the message of redemption provided by Immanuel, and it is the foundational truth throughout the New Testament.

Following his baptism by John the Baptist, Jesus began his public ministry. To his twelve disciples, Jesus spoke privately that he would be crucified and, after three days, he would be raised from the dead. Since Jesus was sinless and perfect as found in the Bible,[16] he had to be more than a mere man: he was God in the flesh. It was this same

---

11 Craig Blomberg, "Matthew," in Gregory K. Beale and Donald A. Carson, eds., *Commentary on the New Testament Use of the Old Testament* (Grand Rapids: Baker Academic, 2008), 5.

12 John 1:14.

13 Its root is *skēnē*, which means a tent or tabernacle.

14 Matthew 1:21.

15 Galatians 4:4.

16 2 Corinthians 5:21: "He made Him who knew no sin...."

Jesus "who knew no sin *to be* sin on our behalf, so that we might become the righteousness of God in Him."[17]

Jesus' prediction of his crucifixion

Knowing that his life would culminate with his death on the cross, Jesus prepared his disciples for his impending crucifixion. "Three versions of Jesus' predictions (Matthew's, Mark's and Luke's) in three locations (Caesarea, Galilee and Judea) make *nine predictions* in the Synoptic Gospels."[18] The most detailed description of Jesus' death was given by him in Judea during the latter days of his ministry. Here is the account as recorded in Mark's Gospel:

> "…and the Son of Man will be delivered to the chief priests and the scribes; and they will condemn Him to death and will hand Him over to the Gentiles. They will mock Him and spit on Him, and scourge Him and kill *Him*, and three days later He will rise again."[19]

Son of Man

In the minds of some people, Son of Man is simply a way of referring to a man belonging to the human race. In eight of the nine predictions,[20] Jesus referred to himself as the Son of Man. "It is a phrase used more frequently than any other (except "Jesus" itself) to refer to Jesus in the Gospels."[21] The term, Son of Man, is never found in the later creeds or confessions of faith. A much deeper messianic meaning comes when one connects Jesus' understanding of the title, Son of Man, with Daniel 7:13–14. The prophet Daniel is describing the Messiah who will establish an everlasting kingdom that "will not

---

17 2 Corinthians 5:21. Italics in the original.

18 Zahniser, *The Mission and Death of Jesus in Islam and Christianity*, 167. Italics not in the original. The nine scriptural references are: Caesarea Philippi (Mark 8:30–33; Matthew 16:20–23; Luke 9:21–22), Galilee (Mark 9:30–32; Matthew 17:22–23; Luke 9:43–45) and Judea (Mark 10:32–34; Matthew 20:17–19; Luke 18: 31–33).

19 Mark 10:33–34. Italics in the original.

20 It was Matthew's account (16:20–23) in which the designation that Jesus was the Son of Man was omitted. It should be noted that in the preceding verses Jesus asked his disciples this question, "Who do people say that the Son of Man is?" (16:13).

21 I. Howard Marshall, "Son of Man" in Green, McKnight and Marshall, eds., *Dictionary of Jesus and the Gospels*, 775. The synoptics mention the term "the Son of Man" 69 times, while the Gospel of John, 13 times.

pass away; And His kingdom is one which will not be destroyed."[22]

Daniel's messianic passage takes on a greater significance when, after being arrested, Jesus stood before the Jewish Sanhedrin. This Council brought forward numerous false witnesses against Jesus. Caiaphas, the high priest, prodded Jesus to answer, but he would not respond. Wanting to end his silence, Caiaphas made this probing declaration: "I adjure (Greek, *exorkizō*) You, by the living God, that You tell us whether You are the Christ, the Son of God."[23]

The word, adjure (*exopkizō* used only here in the New Testament), was deliberately stated as its root is *horkos*, meaning a binding oath. Now Jesus had no choice; he was forced to respond.

> Jesus said to him, "You have said it *yourself*; nevertheless, I tell you, hereafter you will see the Son of Man sitting at the right hand of power, and coming on the clouds of heaven."[24]

The first part of Jesus' reply, "You have said it yourself," could be paraphrased: "Yes, but that's not how I would put it" or "Yes, but I don't mean by that what you mean."[25] Jesus was absolutely agreeing with the high priest that he was indeed the Messiah. It should be noted that the term Messiah or Christ, to most Jews at that time, was thought of as someone who would drive out the Roman interlopers. This idea may have been what the high priest had in mind when he posed the question to Jesus, but such was totally contrary to Jesus' mission. He came not to free the Jewish nation from a foreign invader but to rescue Jews and Gentiles, both sinful by nature, from God's righteous wrath.

In the second part of the statement, Jesus identified himself as the "Son of Man sitting at the right hand of Power, and coming

---

22 Daniel 7:14. "Psalm 80 is another passage with a rather similar 'Son of man' concept: The psalmist prays for God to restore his people" [David Wenham, *Paul: Follower of Jesus or Founder of Christianity?* (Grand Rapids: Eerdmans, 1995), 111].

23 Matthew 26:63.

24 Matthew 26:64. Italics in the original.

25 R.T. France, *The Gospel of Matthew* (Grand Rapids: Eerdmans, 2007), 1027. In Mark's Gospel, Caiaphas uttered a similar challenging query: "Are You the Christ [Messiah], the Son of the Blessed One?" But Jesus' response is more direct: "I am" (*Egō eimi*). See Mark 14:61–62.

with the clouds of heaven" as prophesied by Daniel.[26] Immediately, the high priest charged Jesus with blasphemy. How could this son of a carpenter from Nazareth have the audacity to claim to be the long-awaited Messiah promised by God! In utter horror, he tore his clothes. "A high priest must not normally tear his clothes, not even in mourning for the dead (Lev. 21:10–11); it was an action reserved for extreme cases, and, of course, blasphemy was such an extreme case."[27]

From the perspective of the Sanhedrin, Jesus was absolutely culpable of blasphemy, and such a crime under Jewish law was punishable by death. But there was one problem. These Jewish leaders had no *legal* authority to condemn a person to death. Such a right belonged only to Rome's representative—Pontius Pilate, the prefect of Judea. The task before them was to convince this Roman official that Jesus' heinous crime of blasphemy was deserving of the death penalty.

Scourging

As recorded in the Synoptic Gospels, Jesus told his disciples that he would be mistreated by being mocked, spit upon and then scourged—a ghastly punishment. It is believed that the word "scourging" finds its derivation in the Latin word, *excoriare* meaning *ex* "off" and *corium* "skin." The skin was ripped off or flayed. The Romans, having perfected this harrowing punishment, were able to demoralize the most hardened victim.

> The scourge itself consisted of a short, wooden handle with several 18 to 24 (45 to 60 cm) inch-long straps of leather protruding from it. The ends of these pieces of leather were equipped with sharp, rugged pieces of metal, wire and jagged fragments of bones. This was considered to be one of the most feared and deadly weapons of the Roman world.[28]

---

26 Daniel 7:13–14.

27 Leon Morris, *The Gospel According to Matthew* (Grand Rapids: Eerdmans, 1992), 683.

28 Rick Renner, "Scourged," *Sparkling Gems from the Greek* (April 21, 2016); http://www.renner.org/healing/scourged/ (accessed April 21, 2016).

Scourging was known as "the first death" and served as a preparatory stage for crucifixion. The centurion in charge would allow the two lictors (floggers) to beat the victim until he was on the verge of expiring.

Upon the request of the Jewish crowd, Pilate released the murderous insurrectionist Barabbas. He had Jesus scourged and handed him over to be crucified. The effect of this punishment was so intense that Jesus was unable to carry the crossbar (Latin, *patibulum*) and certainly not the whole cross as is often depicted. The Roman soldiers conscripted a bystander, Simon of Cyrene, to carry it for him to Golgotha, the place where the crucifixion was to take place.[29]

Pontius Pilate and Jesus' crucifixion

For ambitious Romans who wanted to ascend the political ladder known as the *cursus honorum*, there were two prescribed orders to follow: senatorial or equestrian. The senatorial route led to the highest and most esteemed office, that of being a consul. Only young men who were members of the wealthy or patrician families could aspire to attain the senatorial offices. Some of the prominent families were the Julia, Claudia or Fabia; there were about twenty families that controlled the senatorial *cursus honorum*.

The other was *eques* or the equestrian class. To become a member of this order, one had to be appointed by the emperor. Once a family had gained this distinction, it could be passed on to succeeding generations. Quite often, Roman soldiers who had a lengthy and distinguished military career were appointed to this class by the emperor.

Equites were composed of less prominent families—some who were very wealthy but lacked the important political connections. Being an integral part of the Imperial civil service, they were in charge of the police and fire brigades in Rome. But two of the most coveted equestrian posts were the prefect of Egypt and the commander of the Praetorian Guard—the emperor's personal bodyguard. As the history of Rome unfolded, the Praetorian Guard became a powerful force within the empire in determining who would become the next emperor.

---

29 Matthew 27:32.

Caesar Augustus (63 B.C.–A.D. 14)

Augustus reigned over the united Roman empire from 27 B.C. until his death in A.D. 14. It was he who made Judea an Imperial province.

In 63 B.C., Pompey (100 B.C.–48 B.C.), the illustrious Roman general, conquered Palestine. Herod the Great (74 B.C.–4 B.C.) and his son, Archelaus (23 B.C.–*ca.* A.D. 18), became client-rulers under Roman authority during the first century B.C. But in A.D. 6, Caesar Augustus (63 B.C.–A.D. 14) deposed Archelaus and made Judea (with Samaria) an Imperial province. Then he appointed Coponius, an *eques*, to be the first prefect of Judea which now was under his direct rule.

For over seven decades, the Jewish people had chafed under Roman imperialistic rule. Constant tension between these two factions was always near boiling point. The mere presence of this pagan imperial power was "an affront to the God of Israel and culturally and religiously threatening."[30]

Coponius, like subsequent Judean prefects, was very much aware of the volatility of this Imperial province. He also knew that this appointment was at the bottom of the equestrian *cursus honorum*. If, as Roman administrator, he could manage to keep peace and stability in Judea—a challenging assignment, his political future seemed highly promising.

In A.D. 26, Pontius Pilate, the third prefect, was sent out to this hotbed of political intrigue and dissension. It has been speculated that Emperor Tiberius (42 B.C.–A.D. 37) approved his selection as a result of his successful military career. Pilate's prefecture was to last ten years (A.D. 26–36). All that history has recorded about this *eques* is confined to that decade. Any information prior to 26, or especially after his recall by Tiberius in 36, is purely apocryphal.[31]

There are three major sources that outline Pilate's career: Philo, Josephus and the New Testament. They all agree that he was "greedy, inflexible and cruel and one who resorted to robbery and oppression, a portrait not out of keeping with Luke 13:1."[32] Luke's passage states:

---

30 Wenham, *Paul: Follower of Jesus or Founder of Christianity?*, 36.

31 See Warren Carter, *Pontius Pilate: Portraits of a Roman Governor* (Collegeville: Liturgical Press, 1989), 6-11.

32 Harold W. Hoehner, "Chronology," in Green, McKnight and Marshall, eds., *Dictionary of Jesus and the Gospels*, 121.

Now on the same occasion there were some present who reported to Him about the Galileans whose blood Pilate had mixed with their sacrifices.[33]

Historian Helen Bond observed that Pilate, similar to the other prefects of Judea, would have been some obscure name relegated to the pages of Philo and Josephus. "Yet a chance encounter with Jesus of Nazareth ensured that his name survived in Christian recollection. It was one historical event—the trial of Jesus."[34]

During his three-year ministry, the continual theological struggles between himself and the members of the Jewish Sanhedrin inevitably paved the way for Jesus' fateful encounter with Pontius Pilate. On two consecutive occasions as recorded in Luke's Gospel, the scribes and Pharisees challenged Jesus' actions on the Sabbath.[35] First, he never forbade his disciples from picking heads of grain and then eating them on the Jewish day of rest. Some time later on another Sabbath, he healed a man who had a withered hand. The legalistic framework within Judaism had carefully delineated the categories of "work" that were permissible on the Sabbath and Jesus, in both incidents, had flagrantly violated them.

Jesus' healing of a paralytic man and then forgiving his sins caused the scribes to reason: "Why does this man speak that way? He is blaspheming; who can forgive sins but God alone?"[36] Later, Jesus refers to himself as possessing the same divine nature as God the Father when he states: "I and the Father are one."[37] Stating that he was God so incensed the Jewish leaders that they were ready to stone him to death.

Such persistent disregard for Jewish traditions forced the Sanhedrin into action. The ideal time presented itself when Judas Iscariot, a disciple of Jesus, willingly betrayed him. This traitorous follower led the Jewish leaders to the Garden of Gethsemane where they arrested Jesus and later brought him before Pilate. The Sanhedrin

---

33 Luke 13:1

34 Helen K. Bond, *Pontius Pilate in History and Interpretation* (Cambridge: Cambridge University Press, 1998), 206.

35 Luke 6:1-11.

36 Mark 2:7.

37 John 10:30.

Tiberius **(42 B.C.-A.D. 37)**

had no difficulty in laying charges against Jesus. His egregious actions warranted nothing less than the death penalty but, under Roman law, they were totally powerless. Only the prefect, in this case Pilate, had the authority granted by Caesar Augustus to enforce the death penalty on non-Roman provincials.[38]

After Pilate's last dialogue with Jesus, he announced to the Jewish crowd that he found no substantive grounds to have Jesus executed. On the contrary, he felt that this innocent man should be released. Totally appalled by what Pilate suggested, Jesus' accusers felt justified in bringing forth what they considered to be their most devastating tactic:

> If you release this Man, you are no friend of Caesar; everyone who makes himself out *to be* a king opposes Caesar.[39]

This two-fold thrust left Pilate with only one option—to sentence Jesus to death. First, Pilate, like every senator or *eques*, aspired to move up the *cursus honorum*. But promotions "to public office depended not so much on individual competence as connections and influences in the imperial court."[40] The Latin term for "connections and influences" was *clientella* or patrons. To be a member of the emperor's *clientella* made one a "friend of Caesar" (Greek, *philos tou Kaisaros*). Such a relationship ensured one's upward movement on the political ladder. Since Tiberius was responsible for his appointment as prefect of Judea, Pilate was keenly aware that, if the Sanhedrin approached the emperor concerning his release of Jesus, it could possibly mar his years of faithful patronage.

---

38 For further information, see A.N. Sherwin-White, *Roman Society and Roman Law in the New Testament* (Oxford: Clarendon Press, 1965), 5–9.

39 John 19:12. Italics in the original.

40 Bond, *Pontius Pilate in History and Interpretation*, 10–11.

Second, the worship of Roman emperors never took root in the early years of the principate in the West but it did in the Eastern part of the Roman empire. The precedent had been set with the Egyptian worship of the pharaohs and even the deification of Greece's Alexander the Great. Thus, the imperial cult of emperor worship given to Augustus and Tiberius continued with the construction of temples on their behalf.[41] So, it seems entirely reasonable that Pilate could have ordered a place of worship be built for Tiberius. The limestone block found in 1961 could have been a part of that Tiberium.[42] But, if it were reported to Rome that Pilate had tolerated the worship of another king, namely Jesus, instead of Caesar, the temple to honour Tiberius would have become entirely meaningless—Pilate's political career would be in jeopardy.

The Sanhedrin was greatly gratified that they had forced Pilate to crucify Jesus, but their success was only momentary. Pilate struck back. Motivated by retribution, Pilate— ignoring their arduous protestations—ordered an inscription (Greek, *titlos*)[43] to be placed above the cross in Hebrew, Latin and Greek: "JESUS THE NAZARENE, THE KING OF THE JEWS."[44]

The apostle Paul and Jesus' cross

The apostle Paul (born Saul) presented an autobiographical sketch to the church at Philippi, demonstrating that he had been a model Jew:

> ...circumcised the eighth day, of the nation of Israel, of the tribe of Benjamin, a Hebrew of Hebrews; as to the Law, a Pharisee; as to zeal, a persecutor of the church; as to the righteousness which is in the Law, found blameless.[45]

---

41 See Simon Price, *Rituals and Power: The Roman Imperial Cult in Asia Minor* (Cambridge: Cambridge University Press, 1984).

42 Hourihane, *Pontius Pilate, Anti-Semitism and the Passion in Medieval Art*, 41.

43 See Chapman and Schnabel, *Trial and Crucifixion of Jesus*, 292–298. Here, the authors show how the *titulus* (Latin) was used in a horrendous fashion by the maniacal emperors, Gaius Caligula (A.D. 12–41) and Domitian (A.D. 51–96).

44 John 19:19.

45 Philippians 3:5–6.

The first four things Paul mentions were inherited privileges while the last three were personal achievements. His first claim was: "circumcised the eighth day."[46] Born into a Jewish family, Paul was circumcised as prescribed by the commandment of God to Abraham in Genesis 17:11–12. In this way, "he bore in his body the badge and the mark that he was of the chosen of God, marked out by God as His own."[47]

The next two identify Paul as an Israelite of the tribe of Benjamin. He was raised in Tarsus, the capital of Cilicia (today in modern Turkey). It was a thriving economic centre and also a gateway to the east. Using Roman roads, merchants could travel through Tarsus to Syria and down the eastern coast of the Mediterranean Sea to Palestine and even on to Egypt.

Not only was Tarsus known nationally and internationally as a hive of commercial activity, it was a leading philosophical centre. It rivalled the three reputed "universities" of the ancient world: Athens, Alexandria and Rhodes.[48] Strabo, a first century geographer, wrote of the intellectual impact of Tarsus during the first century A.D.:

> But it is Rome that is best able to tell the number of learned men from this city; for it is full of Tarsians and Alexandrians. Such is Tarsus.[49]

Living in a Hellenized city,[50] Paul's father would have wanted to protect his son from the Greek influences that arose through language, customs and culture. He would probably have done so by establishing linguistic, religious and social barriers in order that his son could be known as "a Hebrew of Hebrews." Paul would have spoken only Hebrew or Aramaic at home. At the local synagogue school, he would have read the Old Testament—the Torah—in Hebrew.

---

46 The Greek *okta* (eight) *ēmeros* (day) literally means an eighth-day one.

47 William Barclay, *The Mind of St. Paul* (New York: Harper and Row, 1958), 25.

48 Rhodes, an island in the Aegean Sea, is about 10 km away from the southeast coast of Asia Minor (modern Turkey).

49 Strabo, *Geography* in the Loeb Classical Library, trans. Horace Leonard Jones (Cambridge: Harvard University Press, 1989), 14.5.15.

50 "Hellenized" is from the Greek *hellēnizō*, meaning "to make one a Greek."

The last three credentials concentrate on Paul's personal accomplishments. Possibly in his teens and now a Pharisee by personal conviction, Paul (then Saul) left Tarsus and travelled to Jerusalem in order to be trained by the renowned Pharisee, Gamaliel.[51] For the next three or four years, Paul was undoubtedly motivated by this Pharisaic *bon mot* or witty comment: "An ignorant man cannot be holy."[52]

Thus, Paul poured his energies into mastering the intricacies of both the written and oral traditions of the Torah. Certainly, God authored the first five books of Moses, but the Scriptures, especially the laws, had to be interpreted and applied to life—these became the basis of the oral traditions. In the mind of many Jews, these traditions were accepted on equal footing with the five books of Moses.[53]

The seventh and last credential would have been viewed as the pinnacle of his spiritual pedigree. As a Jew whose entire life was prescribed by the Torah and the oral traditions, he could make the subjective evaluation that he was blameless or without fault (Greek, *amemptos*) before his God.

Having achieved the highest goal in life—the approval of God himself, Paul now felt compelled to convince his fellow Jews who had become followers of Jesus Christ that they had been spiritually duped. "The Christian proclamation of a man who had been crucified as the promised Messiah of Israel must have appeared utterly scandalous."[54] Such zeal, or more accurately, such hatred, caused him to pillage, destroy or annihilate (Greek, *portheō*)[55] these Jewish Christians.

---

51 Acts 22:3.

52 Jerome Murphy-O'Connor, *Paul: A Critical Life* (Oxford: Clarendon Press, 1996), 12.

53 "The words that Moses finally committed to writing in the Torah scroll is called *Torah shebikhtav*. According to this view, there were actually two Torahs given to Moses on Sinai: the written Torah and the oral Torah, and together these are considered the full revelation of the Torah." John Parsons, "Torah sheba'al Peh: the Oral Torah and the Jewish Tradition," *Hebrew for Christians* (no date); http://www.hebrew4christians.com/Articles/Oral_Torah/oral_torah.html (January 2, 2018).

54 Udo Schnelle, *Apostle Paul: His Life and Theology* (Grand Rapids: Baker Academic, 2005), 86.

55 William F. Arndt and F. Wilbur Gingrich, *A Greek-English Lexicon of the New Testament* (Chicago: University of Chicago Press, 1952), 699. See Acts 9:21; Acts 22:4; Galatians 1:13, 23.

Armed with authorization from the high priest in Jerusalem, Paul was determined to inflict severe punishment on the believers in Damascus, Syria. En route, his plans were dramatically altered when he was confronted by Jesus who was to become his resurrected Lord.[56] From that moment on, his primary focus was radically changed. His new orientation concerning life was to be found in the freedom that his crucified Lord provided. "It is an obvious truism to say that the cross stands at the heart of Paul's whole theology."[57]

Even before Paul was converted, the primitive Christian church had quickly formulated a tradition (Greek, *paradosis*) that encapsulated the essentials of their new faith. Some two decades later, the apostle Paul took this long-standing tradition and incorporated it into his letter to the Corinthians:

> For I delivered [*paredōka*][58] to you as of first importance what I also received, that Christ died for our sins according to the Scriptures, and that He was buried, and that He was raised on the third day according to the Scriptures.[59]

The tradition had three easily memorizable theological components: "that Jesus was the Messiah, that he died for his people's sins and that this death of his took place in the fulfilment of prophetic scripture."[60] Equally important is a critical observation made by James Dunn , a highly respected British New Testament scholar and author. He is convinced that the acceptance of Jesus as Messiah developed *within a few months* after his resurrection.[61]

Jesus' crucifixion united the two covenants

To the church in Galatia, the apostle Paul, a Jewish Christian, masterfully demonstrated that the gospel message was the same in both the

---

56 Acts 22: 6–11.

57 N.T. Wright, *What Saint Paul Really Said: Was Paul of Tarsus the Real Founder of Christianity?* (Grand Rapids: Eerdmans, 1997), 46.

58 Its root is *paradidōmi*, meaning to deliver or hand over. *Paradosis* is the nominative form.

59 1 Corinthians 15:3–4.

60 F.F. Bruce, *Paul: Apostle of the Heart Set Free* (Grand Rapids: Eerdmans, 1977), 91.

61 See James D.G. Dunn, *Jesus Remembered* (Grand Rapids: Eerdmans, 2003), 855. Italics not in the original.

Old and New Testaments. His distressing letter to these new Galatian believers warned them that salvation and the Christian life cannot be attained through the keeping of the Mosaic Law. He asked this pointed question: "Did you receive the Spirit by the works of the Law, or by hearing with faith?"[62]

To show the work of the Holy Spirit, Paul referenced Abraham, the father of the faithful. This Old Testament patriarch believed what God said: "And I will make you a great nation, and I will bless you…. And in you all the families of the earth will be blessed."[63]

Paul recognized that the fulfilment of these Abrahamic promises came to the Gentiles who by faith believed that Jesus Christ "redeemed (Greek, *exēgorasen*)[64] [them] from the curse of the Law, having become a curse for [them]."[65] Such a newly acquired freedom had this impact on the body of Gentile Christians. "And if you belong to Christ, then you are Abraham's descendants, heirs according to promise."[66]

The apostle Paul's greatest desire was that all believers would experience, as he did, the power of the resurrected Christ in their daily lives. He writes,

> I have been crucified with Christ; and it is no longer I who live, but Christ lives in me; and the *life* which I now live in the flesh I live by faith in the Son of God, who loved me and gave Himself up for me.[67]

---

62 Galatians 3:2.

63 Genesis 12:2–3.

64 The root word for *exēgorasen* is *agora*—the marketplace. Here "a slave could also be put on the market as a 'commodity'" [David J. Williams, *Paul's Metaphors: Their Context and Character* (Peabody: Hendrickson, 1999), 116]. But Christ entered this sinful world and "purchased (*exēgorasas*) for God with [His] blood men from every tribe and tongue…" (Revelation 5:9).

65 Galatians 3:13.

66 Galatians 3:29

67 Galatians 2:20; italics in original.

CHAPTER 2

Jesus' crucifixion and four non-Christian sources

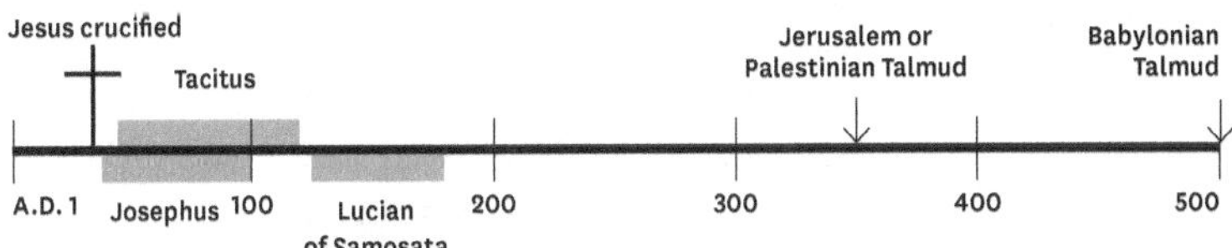

EVEN SCHOLAR BART EHRMAN —"an agnostic with atheist leanings"[1] —felt compelled to pen a book validating the historicity of Jesus. In it, he made this extraordinary and compelling argument concerning Jesus' crucifixion:

> Since no one would have made up the idea of a crucified messiah, Jesus must really have existed, must really have raised messianic expectations, and must really have been crucified.... Paul knew Jesus's right-hand man Peter and Jesus's brother James. They are evidence that this belief in the crucified messiah goes all the way back to a short time after Jesus's death.[2]

---

1 Bart D. Ehrman, *Did Jesus Exist? The Historical Argument for Jesus of Nazareth* (New York: Harper Collins, 2012), 5.

2 Ehrman, *Did Jesus Exist?*, 164.

Beyond the absolute certainty of Jesus' crucifixion as presented in the New Testament, there are four non-biblical sources that also confirm this historical reality. Josephus and Tacitus need special mention as they alone recorded that Jesus' death occurred during the governorship of Pontius Pilate—our historical thread.

Josephus

It is somewhat ironic that a Jewish general who later supported Rome during the Jewish Revolt (A.D. 66-70) would provide compelling evidence for the historicity of another Jew—Jesus of Nazareth. Such was the life of Flavius Josephus. He was born Joseph ben Mattathias from an influential priestly family in Palestine.

In A.D. 64 at the age of twenty-seven, he led a diplomatic mission to Rome where he personally witnessed the grandeur of the Roman empire. So, it is not surprising that, when the Roman army under General Titus Flavius Vespasianus (A.D. 9–79) began the conquest of Palestine, Josephus recognized that any resistance was futile and could even be fatal. Consequently, he joined the ranks of the invaders.

This traitor was well rewarded. "After the war he became a Roman citizen and a writer in the employ of the Flavian emperors Vespasian, Titus and Domitian, living in an apartment in their palaces."[3] In honour of his patrons of three generations, he adopted their name and has become known as Flavius Josephus.

Within the comforts provided by his benefactors, Josephus decided to write historical accounts to extol the virtues of the Jewish people to their Roman conquerors. He also wanted to encourage the Jewish people to live in peace under Roman rule. His two most outstanding books were *The Jewish War* (A.D. 75–80) and *Jewish Antiquities* (A.D. 90s). Both were written in Greek so that they would appeal to the educated Roman aristocracy.

The works of Josephus were copied by the early Christians as they recognized their value in gaining a greater understanding of the historical background of the New Testament world. Jesus of Nazareth was mentioned by Josephus only twice in his *Jewish Antiquities*. In

---

3   Robert Van Voorst, *Jesus Outside the New Testament* (Grand Rapids: Eerdmans, 2000), 81.

Flavius Josephus (A.D. 37–100)

Josephus became an eyewitness to the destruction of Jerusalem after he defected to the invading Roman army. He recorded this horrendous event in his book *The Jewish War*. The early fathers of the church often referred to his writings as he was the most reliable source of ancient Jewish history.

the first instance, Josephus wanted to explain why Herod Agrippa (A.D. 27–*ca.* 93) deposed Ananus, the presiding high priest, from office. Josephus, noting that Ananus was both rash and impetuous, gave this explanation:

> Ananus thought that with Festus [the Roman procurator] dead and Albinus [his replacement] still on his way, he would have his opportunity. Convening the judges of the Sanhedrin, he brought before them a man named *James, the brother of Jesus who was called the Christ* and certain others. He accused them of having transgressed the law, and condemned them to be stoned to death.[4]

In order to correctly identify James which was a very common name (at least five mentioned in his works), Josephus added the further descriptor that he was "the brother of Jesus." But since he had already referred to twelve others by the name Jesus,[5] he had to include "who was called the Christ." To the Jewish audience, the term Christ (Greek, *Christos*) would have been written as "Messiah."

Mainline scholars have concluded that "who was called the Christ" was from the pen of Josephus.

> Neither the NT nor early Christian writers spoke of James of Jerusalem in a matter-of-fact way as "the brother of Jesus" but rather—with reverence we would expect—"the brother of the Lord" or "the brother of the Savior."[6]

The second reference to Jesus by Josephus is much more controversial. Known as the *Testimonium Flavianum*, it was first recorded by the renowned author Eusebius (*ca.* A.D. 260–339) in his *Church*

---

4   Josephus, *The Essential Writings: A Condensation of Jewish Antiquities and The Jewish War,* trans. and ed. Paul L. Maier (Grand Rapids: Kregel, 1988), 276. Italics not in the original.

5   Lawrence Mykytiuk, "Did Jesus Exist? Searching for Evidence Beyond the Bible," *Bible History Daily* (October 12, 2014); http://www.biblicalarchaeology.org/daily/people-cultures-in-the-bible/jesus-historical-jesus/did-jesus-exist/ (accessed September 1, 2016). See the same article in *Biblical Archaeology Review* 41 (January/February 2015): 44–51, 76.

6   John P. Meier, *A Marginal Jew: Rethinking the Historical Jesus,* 4 vols. (New York: Doubleday, 1991), 1:58.

History written in A.D. 326.[7]

> About this time Jesus, a wise man, *if indeed one ought to call him a man*. For he was the achiever of extraordinary deeds and was a teacher of those who accept the truth gladly. He won over many Jews and many of the Greeks. *He was the Messiah.* When he was indicted by the principal men among us and Pilate condemned him to be crucified, those who had come to love him originally did not cease to do so; *for he appeared to them on the third day restored to life, as the prophets of the Deity had foretold these and countless other marvelous things about him.* And the tribe of Christians, so named after him, has not disappeared to this day.

According to John Meier, an American biblical scholar and Roman Catholic priest, the italic portions were not in the original text as noted in his book, *A Marginal Jew: Rethinking the Historical Jesus.*[8] The academic community is almost unanimous[9] that the *Testimonium Flavianum* which Eusebius received had been altered by Christian copyists over the years before him.

The original, written by a dedicated Jew, would not have recorded the favourable Christological statements concerning Jesus. But once the disputed passages were removed, the text showed what a historian would accept: "Jesus' ethical conduct, his following and his crucifixion by the command of Pilate."[10]

Robert Van Voorst acknowledges that Josephus' text, *Testimonium Flavianum*, has presented a challenge to academia over the years because most of its manuscripts date back to the eleventh century. According to Van Voorst, "we are left to examine the context, style and content of this passage to judge its authenticity."[11]

---

7   Eusebius, *The Church History: A New Translation with Commentary*, trans. and ed. Paul L. Maier (Grand Rapids: Kregel, 1999), 46.

8   Meier, *A Marginal Jew*, 1:61.

9   Meier, *A Marginal Jew*, 1:62. See also Raymond Brown, *The Death of Jesus* (New York: Doubleday, 1994), 374.

10   Gary R. Habermas, *The Historical Jesus: Ancient Evidence for the Life of Christ* (Joplin: College Press, 2001), 195–196.

11   Van Voorst, *Jesus Outside the New Testament*, 89.

Following this format, Van Voorst presents a scholarly analysis. He made this important observation. "Josephus's testimony that both Jewish leaders and Pilate were involved in the death of Jesus is remarkable, even striking."[12] No other non-biblical account shows that both the Jewish and Roman leadership were responsible for Jesus' crucifixion.

Van Voorst came to the conclusion that John Meier's rendering of this difficult text does bear the marks of authenticity.

Tacitus

Publius (or Gaius) Cornelius Tacitus is widely recognized as "the greatest Roman historian."[13] He also achieved political greatness when, in A.D. 97, Tacitus reached the highest office in Rome's *cursus honorum*, that of consul. In honour of his political acumen, he was appointed in A.D. 112 as proconsul in Asia Minor, an extremely important Roman province (today known as western Turkey).

Tacitus' writings were extensive: his *Annals* and *Histories* number some thirty volumes. *Annals*, written in A.D. 117, began with the death of Augustus in A.D. 14 and ended with the last year of Nero's life in A.D. 68. It was in his fifteenth volume that Tacitus refers to Nero's treatment of Christians. They became Nero's scapegoats for allegedly starting the great fire in Rome in A.D. 64 and were inflicted with the most vicious punishments.[14]

It was within this context that Tacitus brought together Christians and their leader, "Chrestus" or Christ Jesus. He wrote:

> Nero placed the guilt on others on whom he inflicted extraordinary punishments. These people hated for their shameful vices whom the common people called Christians. The man from whom their name is derived is *Chrestus*, who had been executed during the rule of Tiberius by the procurator Pontius Pilate. These pernicious superstitions had been suppressed for a time,

---

12 Van Voorst, *Jesus Outside the New Testament*, 101. See also Josephus, *Antiquitates Judaicae* 18.63–64 in Chapman and Schnabel, *Trial and Crucifixion of Jesus*, 188.

13 Van Voorst, *Jesus Outside the New Testament*, 39. See "Tacitus on Jesus," *Tekton Apologetics*; http://www.tektonics.org/jesusexist/tacitus.php (accessed September 3, 2016) for a list of modern historians who have nothing but high regard for the work of Tacitus.

14 See a description of the punishments in the Introduction.

but were starting to break out again, not merely in Judea where the disease originated but in the city (of Rome) as well.[15]

Tacitus' text provides three important facts that are pertinent to this study. He identified the time period in which Jesus was crucified by stating that Pontius Pilate was the Roman governor in Judea and Tiberius was the reigning emperor. It was important that this Roman historian mention Pilate because it was he who provided "the historical context for the execution of Jesus, the instigator of the *superstitio* of the Christians."[16] Secondly, even though he did not indicate the manner in which Jesus was executed, Tacitus would have known that non-Roman citizens would have been crucified.

Lastly, he showed nothing but disdain for Christianity—an abominable cult. It originated in the east and had rapidly spread westward. Tacitus' greatest concern with this dangerous superstition was that it spurned "the Roman gods, practices secret and probably nefarious rites and therefore is subversive of the good order of the Roman state."[17]

What historical resources concerning Jesus were available to Tacitus? Since the ancient writers never left any indication where they found their material, only speculative answers can be posed. It would seem reasonable that, since Tacitus was a former senator, he would have access to the *Acta Senatus*, the senatorial archives.

Another possible source with much more promise would be Pliny the Younger (A.D. 61–*ca.* 113), a very close friend and a fellow proconsul who was serving in Asia Minor at the same time as Tacitus. Pliny is best known for his ten books of correspondence that have survived—books one to nine are personal letters, but the tenth has garnered the greatest attention as it is his official correspondence with the emperor Trajan (A.D. 53–117).

Pliny wrote to numerous people but "the most frequently named recipient of Pliny's letters was his friend Tacitus, the orator and historian, with 11 letters."[18] In the last letter to his cherished associate,

---

15 Tacitus, *Annales* 15:44 in Chapman and Schnabel, *Trial and Crucifixion of Jesus*, 192–193.

16 Tacitus, *Annales* 15:44 in Chapman and Schnabel, *Trial and Crucifixion of Jesus*, 196.

17 Meier, *A Marginal Jew*, 1:90.

18 Rex Winsbury, *Pliny the Younger: A Life in Roman Letters* (London: Bloomsbury Academic, 2014), 19.

he wrote: "Whether posterity will give us a thought I do not know, but surely we deserve one…which sounds like boasting but for our application, hard work and regard for future generations."[19]

Even though Pliny the Younger was a lawyer by training, he was introduced to a situation of which he had no previous experience: What legitimate and just punishments should he place on Christians who are brought before him? In a letter to Emperor Trajan, he explained what he did. First, he would ascertain whether they were Christians or not. If they were not, then "they all did reverence to your statue and the images of the gods in the same way as the others and reviled the name of Christ."[20] Those who were Roman citizens and professed to being Christians were treated differently than non-Roman believers—the former were sent to Rome to be tried and the latter were executed.

It is inconceivable that Tacitus would not have been privy to Pliny's interactions with Christians. Thus, through a fellow lawyer and colleague, Tacitus would have gained valuable insight into what Christians believed and, also, the One whom they worshipped as Lord and Saviour.

Lucian of Samosata

Coinciding with the emergence of the fifteenth-century Renaissance was the invention of the printing press in 1453. The availability of the printed works of Lucian of Samosata (*ca.* A.D. 125–180), especially *On the Death of Peregrinus*, delighted Renaissance humanists. This second-century satirist's irreverent attitude toward religion, and more specifically, Christianity, resonated with these scholars as they too were engaged in a hateful battle against the Roman Catholic Church.

In 1559, the Roman Church took action "when several of his works, including [*On the Death of Peregrinus*] was placed on the Catholic Church's newly created[21] *Index Librorum Prohititorum* (Index of Pro-

---

19 Pliny, *Letters and Panegyricus*, trans. Betty Radice, 2 vols. (Cambridge: Harvard University Press, 1976), 2.9.14.

20 Pliny, *Letters and Panegyricus*, 2.10.96.

21 "The first Index of Prohibited Books was established in 1557 by Pope Paul IV in the middle of the Counter-Reformation, as a list of books that Catholics were prohibited from reading on pain of excommunication." D. Sheridan, "The Catholic Case: The Index of Prohibited Books," *Journal of Hindu-Christian Studies* 19 (2006); http://digitalcommons.butler.edu/cgi/viewcontent.cgi?article=1363&context=jhcs (accessed

Trajan (A.D. 53–117)

hibited Books)."[22] By 1590, all of Lucian's works were on the *Index*.

Who was this second-century author whose writings found such an appeal with readers twelve centuries later? Lucian was born in Samosata, located on the Euphrates River in northeast Syria. It was a prominent city that had a "direct trade route from Ephesus [in Asia Minor] to India."[23] As a young man, Lucian left his home country and adopted the Greco-Roman lifestyle and culture. He authored over seventy books, which were written in the common language of the Roman empire—*Koinē* Greek. History has remembered him as the writer of "the best Greek prose known since the days of Plato and Demosthenes."[24]

Lucian's *On the Death of Peregrinus* (*ca.* A.D. 165) has become the most famous and controversial as a result of its negative allusions to Jesus' crucifixion and Christian beliefs. Such was not his original intent. Lucian wrote what was to be an amusing letter to a friend, Cronius, concerning the antics and buffoonery of Peregrinus of Parium (A.D. 110–165), a person of some wealth and influence.

In writing this satire, Lucian recognized that Peregrinus was an ideal choice as he was

> no minor figure whom he plucked from obscurity to be the butt of a learned joke, but a Cynic on whose philosophical, political, and religious pretensions no cultured man could fail to have an opinion.[25]

Interestingly, Lucian's satirical introduction to *On the Death of Peregrinus* began by referring to Peregrinus' suicide on a pyre near the Olympic Games in A.D. 165. More shocking is that the elderly Peregrinus announced four years previously that he would take his own life.

October 9, 2017). The *Index* was abolished in 1966.

22 C.T. Hadavas, *Lucian, On the Death of Peregrinus: An Intermediate Ancient Greek Reader* (no place: C.T. Hadavas, 2014), xiv.

23 Christopher Robinson, *Lucian and His Influence in Europe* (Chapel Hill: The University of North Carolina Press, 1979), 3. Robinson mentioned that Samosata was famous for fruit trees, timber and herbal medicines.

24 Francis G. Allinson, *Lucian: Satirist and Artist* (Boston: Marshall Jones, 1926), 4.

25 Christopher P. Jones, *Culture and Society in Lucian* (Cambridge: Harvard University Press, 1986), 132.

Unlucky Peregrinus, or, as he delighted to style himself Proteus.... After turning into everything for the sake of notoriety and achieving any number of transformations, here at last he turned into fire; so great, was the love of notoriety that possessed him. And now your genial friend has *got himself carbonized.*[26]

Peregrinus was born in Parium located in northwest Turkey on the Hellespont (today the Dardanelles). Little is known of his early life but there is a record of a number of nefarious crimes that he committed. A rumour circulated that he allegedly killed his father in order to take possession of his inheritance.

Wanting to leave this revolting life behind, he went into voluntary exile. Arriving in Palestine, Peregrinus became acquainted with Christians and soon became identified with them. In Lucian's opinion, this intelligent con artist had not changed but took advantage of these unsuspecting Christians whom Lucian described with the following words:

He interpreted and explained some of their books and even composed many, and they received him as a god, made use of him as a lawgiver, and set him down as a protector, next after that other, to be sure, whom they still worship, *the man who was crucified in Palestine* because he introduced this new cult into the world.[27]

But their loyalty toward this man was even heightened when Peregrinus was arrested and imprisoned for violating an imperial decree. Trajan "ordered that Christians should not be hounded, but, if they were formally accused of being a Christian, regular legal proceeding could be started against them."[28] Looking upon Peregrinus as a martyr, the Christian community dutifully met all his needs whom they called their "new Socrates."[29] News spread of his impris-

---

26 Lucian, "The Passing of Peregrinus," trans. A.M. Harmon in *The Loeb Classical Library*, 8 vols. (Cambridge: Harvard University Press, 1955), 5:3. Italics added.

27 Lucian, "The Passing of Peregrinus," 5:13. Italics added.

28 Stephen Benko, *Pagan Rome and the Early Christians* (Bloomington: Indiana University Press, 1984), 30.

29 Lucian, "The Passing of Peregrinus," 5:13.

onment and Christian congregations as far as Asia Minor were sending him both material and financial aid.

Lucian's reaction to these duped Christians was predictable:

The poor wretches have convinced themselves, first and foremost, that they were going to be immortal and live for all time, in consequence of which they despise death and even willingly give themselves into custody, most of them. Furthermore, their first lawgiver [Christ][30] persuaded them that they are all brothers of one another after they have transgressed once for all by denying the Greek gods and *by worshiping that crucified sophist* himself and living under the laws.[31]

Even though Lucian saw Christianity through second-century Greek eyes with his various misconceptions, "his knowledge, however it was acquired, was on some points surprisingly exact."[32] He noted that the Christians of his day denied the Greco-Roman gods with some paying the ultimate price—their lives. But they faced death with confidence that they had eternal life.

Lucian also recognized their deep respect for their own scriptures and brotherly love for one another. But most importantly, Lucian made two references to their belief in a crucified Messiah. In the second, he referred to Jesus as a "sophist"—a title never applied to Jesus in the New Testament. Lucian's usage of this term was a reflection of his understanding of Greek philosophy. "In the second century, the derisive label 'sophist' was aimed at one who taught only for money and who could at times also be labeled, like Peregrinus, a 'cheat.'"[33] Such a designation could never be used of Jesus Christ.

As a satirist, Lucian's main objective was to show the destructive power of pride. But even though he had nothing but contempt for Christianity—not unlike the majority of his contemporaries—he was

---

30 A.M. Harmon, the translator, made this comment: "From the wording of this sentence the allusion is so obviously to Christ himself that one is at a loss to understand why Paul, let alone Moses, should have been suggested. For the doctrine of brotherly love cf. Matt. 23:8." Lucian, "The Passing of Peregrinus," 5:15, n.1.

31 Lucian, "The Passing of Peregrinus," 5:15. Italics added.

32 Benko, *Pagan Rome and the Early Christians*, 122. See also, Van Voorst, *Jesus Outside the New Testament*, 60.

33 Van Voorst, *Jesus Outside the New Testament*, 62.

able to demonstrate what was believed by second-century Christians regarding Jesus: he had indeed been crucified!

The Babylonian Talmud[34]

Did *b. Sanhredrin 43a*, a passage in the Babylonian Talmud, make a direct reference to Jesus and, more specifically, his crucifixion or not? Different opinions have emerged. In *New Testament Studies*, a highly reputable theological journal, two internationally recognized scholars, Lou Silberman (1915–2006) and Raymond Brown (1928–1998), debated this issue.

Silberman, a former Jewish professor at Vanderbilt University, was extremely skeptical that the Talmud would have made any mention of Jesus.[35] Contrarily, Brown, a former New Testament scholar, disagreed.[36]

Peter Schäfer (1943–), professor emeritus in Judaic studies at Princeton University and a prolific author, has written a definitive study, *Jesus in the Talmud*, in defence of Raymond Brown's position. He maintained: "Within the vast corpus of rabbinic literature, we find but one reference to Jesus' trial and execution."[37] It is *b. Sanhedrin 43a*, as cited below:

> It was taught: On the Eve of Passover they hanged *Yeshu the Notzri* [Nazarene]. And the herald went out before him for forty days (before the execution took place [saying]. "*Yeshu the Notzri* will go out to be stoned for sorcery and misleading and enticing Israel [to idolatry]. Anyone who can say anything in his favor, let him come forward and plead on his behalf." But no one came, so they hung him on the Eve of the Passover!

---

34 After the destruction of Jerusalem and the temple by the Romans in A.D. 70, the Pharisees codified their legal traditions into what is known as the Mishnah. "The Mishnah itself became a subject of new case law and theological development. Two Gemaras or 'commentaries' on the Mishnah developed [into the Talmud], one in Palestine…one in Babylon." Van Voorst, *Jesus Outside the New Testament*, 107.

35 Lou H. Silberman, "Once Again: The Use of Rabbinic Material," *New Testament Studies* 42 (1996): 153–155.

36 Raymond Edward Brown, "The Babylonian Talmud on the Execution of Jesus," *New Testament Studies* 43 (1997): 158–59.

37 Peter Schäfer, *Jesus in the Talmud* (Princeton: Princeton University Press, 2007), 63.

Ulla said, "Do you suppose that the Notzri was one for whom a defense could be made? He was a deceiver," and the Merciful says, "You shall not spare and you shall not shield him (Deut. 13:9). With *Yeshu the Notriz*, however, it was different, for he was close to the government."[38]

The main message of *b. Sanhedrin 43a* focused upon the legal procedure of sending out a herald (Greek, *kārux*) to announce the death penalty which had been pronounced on a convicted criminal. Such a practice was clearly set forth in *m. Sanhedrin 6:1*. It stated:

When sentence [of death penalty] has been passed, they take him out to stone him…. A herald goes out before him, calling "So-and-so, the son of so-and-so, is going to be stoned because he committed such-and-such a transgression. So-and-so are witnesses against him. If anyone knows something [that is grounds] for acquittal, let him come and speak on his behalf."[39]

In *b. Sanhedrin 43a*, the declaration was concerning Jesus of Nazareth. The Talmud specifically stated that a herald was sent out forty days before the actual crucifixion. Even though the New Testament never specified that Jesus' execution was proclaimed for forty days, Van Voorst has put forth this suggestion to reconcile the two accounts.[40] He noted that in John 11:45–51, after Jesus had raised his friend Lazarus from the dead, the Sanhedrin, the Jewish highest court, began to plot how they could kill Jesus. "So from that day on they planned together to kill him."[41] Thus in actuality, Jesus' arrest was set into motion weeks before he was apprehended.

The charge against Jesus according to the Talmud was committing sorcery. The New Testament never stated this crime. Instead, the Jews on four occasions as recorded in the Gospel of John accused

---

38 Babylonian Talmud, *b. Sanhedrin 43a* in Chapman and Schnabel, *Trial and Crucifixion of Jesus*, 136–137. See a later rendition, Babylonian Talmud, *Sanhedrin 43a*, 4 vols. (London, England: The Soncino Press, 1935), 3:281–282. Italics added.

39 Babylonian Talmud, *m. Sanhedrin 6:1* in Chapman and Schnabel, *Trial and Crucifixion of Jesus*, 58–59.

40 Van Voorst, *Jesus Outside the New Testament*, 118.

41 John 11:53.

Jesus of being demon-possessed and insane.[42] Also, one of the witnesses claimed that Jesus said: "I am able to destroy this temple of God and to rebuild it in three days."[43] Schäfer said that the Talmud editors would have no difficulty in deeming this act as sorcery.[44]

Both the New Testament and this Talmudic account have total agreement on two important matters. First, they both reported that Jesus' death occurred on the eve of the Passover.[45] Secondly, there is unanimity in the terminology used to describe Jesus' crucifixion. They mentioned that he was hanged. The apostle Paul wrote: "Christ redeemed us from the curse of the Law, having become a curse for us—for it is written, "CURSED IS EVERYONE WHO HANGS ON A TREE.""[46]

Schäfer's chapter titled "Jesus' Execution" summarized the importance of *b. Sanhedrin 43a* from a Jewish perspective. This passage has removed, once for all, the necessity for justifying their involvement in Jesus' death. Their shame or guilt are gone as they have taken full responsibility. Furthermore, they "even convinced the Roman governor (or more precisely: forced him to accept) that this heretic and impostor needed to be executed—and we are proud of it."[47]

Conclusion

These four diverse descriptions of Jesus' crucifixion add greater credibility to the already trustworthy accounts of the New Testament. With the growth of Christianity beyond the first two centuries, the testimony of the early church fathers has given even more credence to the undeniable reality of the crucifixion of Jesus and his subsequent resurrection.

---

42 John 10:20. The other three were John 7:20; 8:48, 52.

43 Matthew 26:61; Mark 14:58.

44 Schäfer, *Jesus in the Talmud*, 69.

45 John 19:14 states: "Now it was the day of preparation for the Passover; it was about the sixth hour."

46 Galatians 3:13.

47 Schäfer, *Jesus in the Talmud*, 74.

Statue of Zeus at Olympia

The Olympian Zeus was one of the Seven Wonders of the Ancient World. It was constructed around 435 B.C. and stood over 40 feet tall.

CHAPTER 3

The witness to Jesus' crucifixion by the early church fathers

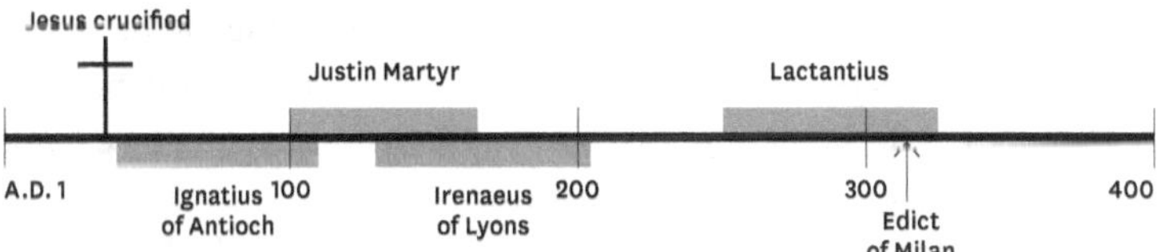

Christianity branded as atheism

PLINY THE YOUNGER, proconsul of Bithynia-Pontus, wanting to bless the emperor, "offered prayers to the gods to keep him in health and prosperity *on behalf of the human race,* whose security and happiness depend on his safety."[1]

The Roman populous sincerely believed that it was only through the beneficence of the gods that they could experience peace and security. Honouring the gods pervaded every aspect of their lives. All public and private religious ceremonies and activities began with an acknowledgment of the gods. The Olympic Games, a lasting tribute from the ancient world, were dedicated to Zeus, the supreme deity.

---

1 Pliny, *Letters and Panegyricus*, 2.10.52. Italics added. See 2.10.35 for the people's vows for the emperor at the beginning of every year.

With certainty, it could be said: "To be Roman was to be religious."[2]

Even though the gods were extremely human in their actions in that they ate, drank, lied, cheated and "otherwise set morally unedifying examples,"[3] to ignore and anger them would spell utter disaster. The general populace believed the gods had power to invoke catastrophes such as violent storms or virulent plagues.

Within the context of this perpetual fear, Romans were faced with another problem: Christians! It was they who had the audacity to openly state that these gods did not exist. This denial incensed the pagan worshippers and they retaliated by scornfully calling Christianity a superstition (Latin, *superstitio*).

The main objective of religion (Latin, *religio*) for the Romans was to find the proper balance between appeasing the gods and getting blessings from them. By denying the existence of these pagan deities, Christianity was threatening the all-important equilibrium needed to maintain harmony between the gods and the people.

Tacitus and Pliny endorsed the principles of *religio* and had nothing but contempt for Christianity. They believed it was a scourge that was rapidly spreading throughout the world and needed to be exterminated. Tacitus referred to Christianity as "pernicious superstition (*superstitio*)."[4] In the same vein, Pliny expressed his feeling by calling it "a degenerate sort of cult (*superstitionem*)."[5]

Within this hostile religious climate, the accusation of atheism was leveled against Christians—and persecution swiftly followed, even though there was no Roman legislation at the time that forbade one from being a Christian.[6]

So what was their crime? They had deliberately contravened the tradition of the elders (Latin, *mos maiorum*). They "threatened the established order of things, that compact between the ancestral gods of Rome and the Roman people."[7] Two hundred years later, the

---

2   George Heyman, *The Power of Sacrifice: Roman and Christian Discourses in Conflict* (Washington: The Catholic University of America Press, 2007), 43.

3   Rodney Stark, *The Triumph of Christianity: How the Jesus Movement Became the World's Largest Religion* (New York: HarperOne, 2011), 11.

4   Tacitus, *Annales* 15:44 in Chapman and Schnabel, *Trial and Crucifixion of Jesus*, 193.

5   Pliny, *Letters and Panegyricus*, 2.10.56.

6   A close examination of the dialogue between Emperor Trajan and Pliny, who also was a lawyer, reveals that neither seemed to be aware of any law against Christianity.

7   Winsbury, *Pliny the Younger*, 214.

situation would change drastically. Both emperors Decius (A.D. 201–251) and Diocletian (A.D. 244–311) would make Christianity illegal in the Roman empire.

Ignatius of Antioch

"By your denial of the ancestral gods, you, as a Christian, are responsible for this devastating earthquake"[8] might have been the charge leveled against Ignatius of Antioch by the emperor, Trajan. Around A.D. 115, Trajan had his headquarters stationed in Antioch as he was preparing for a war against the Parthians.[9] According to a letter that Ignatius later sent to the church in Rome,[10] it would appear that he had already been condemned to death by Trajan before he left Antioch for Rome.

Ten Roman guards or "ten leopards"[11]—as Ignatius called them—were commissioned to escort Ignatius and others to Rome. Travelling across Asia Minor, they made numerous stops but the one at Smyrna was highly significant. Here, Ignatius received a warm welcome from the young bishop, Polycarp (A.D. 69–155), and his congregation. Knowing

Ignatius of Antioch
(ca. A.D. 35–115)

Born just two years after the crucifixion of Jesus, Ignatius is an important figure in the early history of the church. He spent time with Polycarp in Smyrna and sent letters to the apostolic churches. He was martyred for his faith in A.D. 115 at the Colosseum in Rome.

---

8   Allen Brent, *Ignatius of Antioch: A Martyr Bishop and the Origin of the Episcopacy* (New York: Continuum, 2007), 20.

9   Winsbury, *Pliny the Younger*, 206.

10   "Letters of Ignatius to the Romans," 1.4.3, in *The Apostolic Fathers*, ed. and trans. Bart D. Ehrman, 2 vols. (Cambridge: Harvard University Press, 2003), vol.1. Ehrman also hypothesized that Ignatius was sent as "a 'gift' by the Syrian governor, a criminal donated for the violent hunting games of the Roman amphitheater." Introduction to the "Letters of Ignatius," 1:209.

11   "Letters of Ignatius to the Romans," 1.5.1 in Ehrman, ed., *The Apostolic Fathers*, vol.1.

that Ignatius would be martryed in Rome, they expressed their heart-felt grief and God's blessing upon him.

In response to church delegates who journeyed from Ephesus, Magnesia and Tralles to meet with him, Ignatius sent letters to these three churches to strengthen their faith. He also addressed a letter to the church in Rome in which he instructed them not to interfere in any way with his impending death. "Allow me to be bread for the wild beasts; through them I am able to attain God."[12]

Travelling northwest along the coast of the Aegean Sea, the Roman guards led their captives to the seaport of Troas. Here, Ignatius dispatched three more letters: to the churches at Smyrna and Philadelphia and to Polycarp.

Ignatius' *To the Smyrneans* demonstrates the depth of his theological understanding, as illustrated by the following excerpt:

> For you are fully convinced about our Lord (Greek, *kurios*), that he was *truly* from the family of David according to the flesh, Son of God according to the will and power of God, *truly* born from a virgin and baptized by John.... In the time of Pontius Pilate and the tetrarch Herod, he was *truly* nailed for us in the flesh...so that through his resurrection he might eternally lift up the standard for his holy and faithful ones.[13]

This passage took direct aim against Docetism from which the Greek *dokein* means "to seem." This heresy taught that Jesus "did not have a real or natural body during his life on earth but only an apparent or phantom one."[14] The rationale was that all matter was viewed as evil and anything spiritual was deemed good. The proponents of Docetism argued that it was impossible for the pure and holy Son of God to be enveloped in evil flesh. Thus, during his earthly ministry, Jesus only "seemed" to possess an earthly body. Furthermore, his sufferings on the cross were totally imaginary.

---

12 "Letters of Ignatius to the Romans," 1.4.1 in Ehrman, ed., *The Apostolic Fathers*, vol.1.

13 "Letters of Ignatius to the Smyrneans," 1.1.1–2 in Ehrman, ed., *The Apostolic Fathers*, vol.1. Italics added.

14 "Docetism" in *Encyclopedia Britannica* (2016); https://www.britannica.com/topic/Docetism (accessed September 20, 2016).

In his denunciation of this false teaching, Ignatius declared that Jesus was Lord (Greek, *kurios*),[15] the God-man, the perfect unity of both the divine and the human. To illustrate "the centrality afforded the incarnation and crucifixion of Jesus Christ"[16] and to completely dismantle Docetism, Ignatius used the word "truly" three times. It is a translation from the Greek *alēthōs*, which is related to *alētheia* meaning truth or verity.

His first declaration of truth was that Jesus was born of the lineage of David, a fact which had been well established in the New Testament and prophesied in the Old. Secondly, he attested to Jesus' miraculous birth. Finally, he linked historically the Saviour's crucifixion to the time period in which Pontius Pilate[17] and Herod the tetrarch lived.

Ignatius' martyrdom in A.D. 115 highlights the spiritual battle between Christianity and Roman paganism. Empowered by Jesus, the resurrected Lord, he entered the Colosseum in Rome and gained victory over death—a hope not found in ancient paganism. Géza Vermes (1924–2013), an authority on early Christianity, wrote that the letters of Ignatius were "a rich mine for the investigation of early Christian thought."[18]

Justin Martyr

In his three works[19] Justin Martyr covers a large part of the theological field. Christianity was for him the highest truth, the crown of both Greek philosophy and Jewish scriptures.[20]

---

15 "Like the New Testament authors, Ignatius refers to Jesus as 'the Lord' (over thirty times) and 'Son of God' (six times), but unlike many of them, he does not hesitate to refer to Jesus as 'our God' and 'my God.'" Gregory Vall, *Learning Christ: Ignatius of Antioch and the Mystery of Redemption* (Washington: The Catholic University of America Press, 2013), 97.

16 William R. Schoedel, *Ignatius of Antioch: A Commentary on the Letters of Ignatius of Antioch* (Philadelphia: Fortress, 1985), 17.

17 There are two other references to Pontius Pilate: "Letters of Ignatius to the Trallians," 1.1.9 and "Letters of Ignatius to the Magnesians," 1.1.11 in *The Apostolic Fathers*, vol.1.

18 Géza Vermes, *Christian Beginnings: From Nazareth to Nicaea* A.D. *30–325* (New York: Penguin, 2013), 165.

19 His three books are: *First Apology*, *Second Apology* and *Dialogue with Trypho*.

20 L.W. Barnard, *Justin Martyr: His Life and Thought* (Cambridge: Cambridge University Press, 1967), 26.

As a young man, Justin Martyr "set out to reach the truth; to gain a perfect knowledge of God was his greatest and only ambition."[21] He attained his greatest desire when he met an elderly man who pointed him to the Scriptures, especially to the writings of the prophets. After that encounter, Justin never saw the man again but

> my spirit was immediately set on fire, and affection for the prophets and for those who are friends of Christ, took hold of me.... Furthermore, it was my wish that everyone would be of the same sentiments as I.[22]

Now committed to Christ, Justin became an ardent defender and apologist of his newfound faith in the public forum. His first defence or *Apology* was addressed to the emperor Antonius Pius (A.D. 86–161) and written while Justin was living in Rome around A.D. 157. Who was this man who had the audacity to challenge the emperor with a lengthy defence of Christianity in the Roman empire?

Justin was born in Flavia Neapolis in Palestine. During the reign of Titus, Justin's parents settled in this new Roman colony with the promise of gaining Roman citizenship. Even though Justin grew up in a remote area of the Roman empire, he dreamed of being a professional philosopher. He truly believed that "philosophy was indeed one's greatest possession, and was most precious in the sight of God."[23]

Some time later (the exact date is unknown), Justin travelled to Rome to set up a Christian philosophical school. Students "came from far and wide to sit at the feet of the renowned teacher and there learn the rudiments of a Christian philosophy."[24] Two of his most famous students were Tatian (A.D. 110–172) and Irenaeus of Lyons who had sat under the ministry of Polycarp.

Justin confronted Roman society with the gospel of Jesus Christ. His *Dialogue with Trypho*, a Christian witnessing to a Jewish friend, adequately demonstrates this point. Here he challenges society's

---

21 Justin Martyr, *Writings of Justin Martyr* in *The Fathers of the Church*, vol. 9, trans. Thomas B. Falls (New York: Christian Heritage, 1948), 10.

22 Martyr, *Dialogue with Trypho* in vol. 9, *The Fathers of the Church*, 8.

23 Martyr, *Dialogue with Trypho* in vol. 9, *The Fathers of the Church*, 2.

24 Barnard, *Justin Martyr: His Life and Thought*, 13.

misconception that Christians who did not believe in the existence of the pagan gods must be atheists. Justin argued that this view was baseless. "What sober-minded person then will not admit that we are not atheists, since we worship the Maker of the universe."[25]

Unlike the ancient philosophers who sought understanding for the meaning of life by means of human logic, Justin called upon a greater source—*divine revelation*. For him, they were the Jewish and Christian writings. It would be at least fifty years—during the time of Tertullan (*ca.* A.D. 150–220), the renowned theologian of Carthage— that the Jewish and Christian writings would become known as the Old and New Testaments.[26]

Justin Martyr (A.D. 100–165)

A teacher of Christian philosophy, Justin confronted Roman society with the gospel of Jesus Christ and called people to a greater source of understanding—through divine revelation. He was eventually martyred for his faith in A.D. 165.

Justin had complete scrolls for the majority of the Old Testament but he was partial to Genesis, Isaiah and the Psalms.[27] However, to understand the historical setting and the spiritual implications of Jesus' crucifixion, he relied on the *Memoirs* or the *Remembrances of Jesus*, known today as the Gospels. "There is no reason to doubt that Justin made extensive use of Paul's letters, especially Romans and Galatians."[28] In his *First Apology*, he wrote,

> Our Teacher of these things is Jesus, who was born for this end, and who was crucified under Pontius Pilate, the procurator of Judea, in the reign of Tiberius Caesar. We shall prove that we worship Him with reason, since we have learned that He is the Son of the living God Himself.[29]

---

25 Justin Martyr, *The First and Second Apologies*, Ancient Christian Writers, trans. L.W. Barnard (New York: Paulist Press, 1997), 13.

26 Oskar Skarsaune, "Justin and His Bible," in *Justin Martyr and His Worlds*, eds. S. Parvis and P. Foster (Minneapolis: Fortress, 2007), 54.

27 Skarsaune, "Justin and His Bible," in Parvis and Foster, eds., *Justin Martyr and His Worlds*, 57–58.

28 Skarsaune, "Justin and His Bible," in Parvis and Foster, eds., *Justin Martyr and His Worlds*, 4.

29 Martyr, *The First and Second Apologies*, 13.

Wanting to show the historicity of Jesus' crucifixion, Justin identified Pontius Pilate as the governor of Judea who represented the Roman emperor Tiberius. In his three major works, Justin referred to Pilate nine times.[30]

In A.D. 161, Marcus Aurelius (A.D. 121–180) became emperor. He was opposed to Christianity and took aggressive steps against it. Since Justin was an outspoken Christian apologist, it is not surprising that he was brought before Roman officials and found guilty of demeaning the ancestral gods.

> After a brave refusal to sacrifice [to the gods], Justin and those with him are condemned to be beaten with rods and beheaded. They pass to their death praising God and confessing Christ.[31]

Irenaeus of Lyons

Irenaeus was considered to be "the greatest theologian to arise in the Church since the time of the apostles."[32] Unlike earlier Christian apologists, his main source for refuting false teaching was the Bible, rather than philosophy. "Irenaeus believed that reliance on human reason (philosophy) resulted in heresy; so for him, the Christian faith must be founded on divine revelation as opposed to human reason."[33]

Irenaeus was born in Smyrna and had the privilege of being mentored by Polycarp, the bishop of the church in his hometown. Later in his classic book, *Against Heresies*, Irenaeus recalled the impact the early apostles had on his pastor:

> Further, Polycarp was instructed by the apostles [especially, the apostle John][34] and conversed with many who had seen Christ; the apostles in Asia appointed him bishop of the church in

---

30 Martyr, *The First Apology* in Martyr, *The First and Second Apologies*, 13, 35, 46, 48, 61; *The Second Apology* in Martyr, *The First and Second Apologies*, 6; *Dialogue with Trypho*, in Martyr, *The First and Second Apologies*, 30, 76, 85.

31 Barnard, *Justin Martyr: His Life and Thought*, 7.

32 James R. Payton Jr., *Irenaeus on the Christian Faith: A Condensation of Against Heresies* (Cambridge: James Clarke, 2012), ix.

33 James L. Papandrea, *Reading the Early Church Fathers: From Didache to Nicaea* (New York: Paulist Press, 2011), 92.

34 Eusebius, *The Church History*, 5.20.

Smyrna. I also saw him in my early youth, for he lived a long time. As a very old man, he endured a glorious and noble martyrdom and departed this life.[35]

After a number of years of ministering in Smyrna, Irenaeus joined Pothinus (*ca.* A.D. 87–177), another former student of Polycarp,[36] to assist in ministering at the church at Lyons, France. Located on the Rhone River, Lyons was also "the converging point for all traffic and trade within Gaul."[37] Since it was the hub of economic activity, it would seem natural that those who were emigrating from the east would choose this French city in which to settle.

Irenaeus was well-suited for his ministerial role in Lyons. As Pothinus' assistant, he was sent to Rome on two occasions to consult Eleutherus (d. *ca.* A.D. 185), bishop of Rome, on theological issues. During his absence from Lyons, on his second trip in A.D. 177 as

Irenaeus of Lyons
(*ca.* A.D. 130–202)

Irenaeus' classic work, *Against Heresies*, refuted various heretical teachings such as Gnosticism and defended the scriptural authority and unity of both the Old and New Testaments.

the church's emissary, persecution erupted and Pothinus and other Christians were put to death. On his return to Lyons, Irenaeus was chosen to succeed Pothinus. He faithfully served this church until his martyrdom in A.D. 202.

Around A.D. 180, Irenaeus received a letter from a friend who asked him to write a discourse against the heresy of Valentinus (*ca.* A.D. 100–160). Over the next six years, he wrote five books under the title, *The Detection and Refutation of False Knowledge*[38] (the English

---

35 Irenaeus, *Against Heresies* 3.3.4 (orthodoxebooks, n.d.); http://www.orthodoxe-books.org/node/250 (accessed October 10, 2016). To modernize the English version, I used Payton Jr., *Irenaeus on the Christian Faith*, 58.

36 Payton Jr., *Irenaeus on the Christian Faith*, 2.

37 D. Jeffrey Bingham, "Irenaeus of Lyons," in *The Routledge Companion to Early Christian Thought*, ed. D. Jeffrey Bingham (London: Routledge, 2010), 138.

38 Irenaeus, *Against Heresies*, 4. Preface.1.

title has been changed to *Against Heresies*). Even though Irenaeus had originally placed his sights on the false teaching of Valentinus, he used the term "Gnosticism" to encompass the different heretical groups.

In the Preface to his first book, he stated his purpose for writing against these prevalent heresies:

> Some people have been setting the truth aside in favor of myths and endless genealogies…. Through their subtly concocted arguments they seduce the minds of the inexperienced and take them captive. They deal unfaithfully with the oracles of God [the Bible] and show that they are bad interpreters of the good word of revelation.[39]

The five books of *Against Heresies* could be subdivided into two main sections. The first, comprising of the first two books, dealt specifically with Gnosticism. Irenaeus rejected the Gnostic idea that creation came about through various emanations or series of developments; these, in turn, formed the Demiurge—the master artisan—that brought everything into existence.

Instead, he believed:

> There is one only God, the creator—which is above every principality and power and dominion and virtue. He is Father, he is God, the founder, the maker, the creator who made those things by himself.[40]

Against Heresies was definitely not the only discourse against Gnosticism, but it was "the first post-apostolic, largest and most imposing of these responses."[41] Irenaeus' work was so persuasive that, during the next century, this false teaching was rejected by the Christian community and subsequently died out.

The final three books made up the second section. It was here

---

39 Irenaeus, *Against Heresies*, 1. Preface.1. See, Payton Jr., *Irenaeus on the Christian Faith*, 27.

40 Irenaeus, *Against Heresies*, 2.30.9. See, Payton Jr., *Irenaeus on the Christian Faith*, 51.

41 Payton Jr., *Irenaeus on the Christian Faith*, 6. See also Irenaeus, *Against Heresies* 4.6.2; here, Irenaeus mentioned that Justin Martyr had been writing against Marcion of Pontus.

that Irenaeus' ingenuity as a biblical theologian was on display. He portrayed Jesus Christ, the God-man, whose sole purpose was to provide redemption for a rebellious and fallen humanity. In describing the redemptive work of Christ, Irenaeus coined the term "recapitulation."

Irenaeus based this new theological term on the scriptural teaching of Romans 5 and 1 Corinthians 15. The apostle Paul was drawing a contrast between the first Adam and the last Adam—Jesus Christ. To the Corinthians, he wrote: "So also it is written, 'The first MAN, Adam, BECAME A LIVING SOUL.' The last Adam *became* a life-giving spirit."[42]

It was Adam, the first "head" of humanity, who—under Satan's deception—sinned. Through this act of rebellion, he lost his original intimacy with God. To restore this fellowship, Irenaeus' explanation was:

> What he appeared to be he also was: God recapitulated in himself the ancient formation of man, so that he might kill sin, deprive death of its power, and give life again to humankind.[43]

This recapitulation could have occurred only through Jesus' incarnation—God becoming man.

> Satan defeated Adam through disobedience by means of a tree; Christ defeated Satan by his obedience unto death on the tree of the cross.[44]

Like Ignatius of Antioch and Justin Martyr, Irenaeus had a sense of the importance of history. In denouncing the heresy of Marcion of Pontus, a second-century theologian, Irenaeus noted that Jesus lived "in Judea in the times of Pontius Pilate the governor who was a procurator of Tiberius Caesar."[45] As expected, Irenaeus specifically

---

42 1 Corinthians 15:45. Italics in the original.

43 Irenaeus, *Against Heresies*, 3.18.7. See, Payton Jr., *Irenaeus on the Christian Faith*, 74.

44 D. Minns, "Irenaeus," in *Early Christian Thinkers: The Lives and Legacies of Twelve Key Figures*, ed. Paul Foster (Grand Rapids: IVP Academic, 2011), 47.

45 Irenaeus, *Against Heresies*, 1.27.2. He also mentions Emperor Tiberius in 4.6.2 and 4.22.2.

referred to Pontius Pilate who was closely associated with Jesus' death on the cross.

> ...through Christ Jesus, the Son of God; who because of His surpassing love towards his creation condescended to be born of a virgin, thus uniting humanity in himself to God, and having suffered under Pontius Pilate, and rising again, and having been received up in splendor, he will come again.[46]

Irenaeus, an eminent biblicist, made numerous references to both the Old and New Testaments.[47] Its transforming message of salvation gave him the biblical authority to confront the devastating heresies of the second century A.D. One should not forget that his spiritual legacy was built upon his predecessors: Pothinus, Polycarp and the apostle John.

Lactantius

Little is known about Lactantius' early life. He was born to pagan parents in North Africa. As a young person, he was tutored by Arnobius (d. *ca.* 330) in Sicca Veneria, an important city in Numidia, North Africa. Recognized as a brilliant apologist and ardent critic of paganism,[48] Arnobius introduced Lactantius to the Latin classics. Those written by Cicero "had the greatest and deepest influence on Lactantius both as a stylist and as a thinker."[49]

Around A.D. 300, as a middle-aged man, Lactantius was offered a teaching position in the court of Emperor Diocletian in Nicomedia, the capital of the eastern empire. Since Lactantius was proficient in Latin, the official administrative language of the Roman empire, his linguistic talents were in great demand. Interestingly, Constantine,

---

46 Irenaeus, *Against Heresies*, 3.4.2. See, Payton Jr., *Irenaeus on the Christian Faith*, 60. Pontius Pilate was referred to eight times more.

47 "The only books eventually received in the NT canon that Irenaeus did not quote or allude to were Philemon and 3 John," Payton Jr., *Irenaeus on the Christian Faith*, xiii, n.8.

48 For an account of the life and work of Arnobius, see Claudio Moreschini and Enrico Norelli, *Early Christian Greek and Latin Literature: A Literary History*, trans. Matthew O'Connell (Peabody: Hendrickson, 2005), 392–396.

49 R.M. Ogilvie, *The Library of Lactantius* (Oxford: Clarendon Press, 1978), 58.

later to be sole Roman emperor, was also a member of Diocletian's court at that time; he was being groomed in military and literary studies.

In A.D. 303, Diocletian was urged by members of his court—especially by his associate ruler Galerius (*ca.* A.D. 260–311)—to take action against the Christians. Indeed, the gods had also been consulted. "The response came that the God of the Christians was an enemy of the divine religion."[50] Consequently, the longest and most violent persecution against Christians was initiated. It has come to be known as the Great Persecution (A.D. 303–311).

On February 23, 303, during the observance of *Terminalia* (end of the calendar year), severe measures were enacted against Christians. Diocletian and Galerius

> celebrated this festival by restricting Christian worship, first by burning the scriptures and leveling the churches, next by depriving Christians of their civil rights, and within a month by compelling everyone to sacrifice to the gods or risk imprisonment, torture and death.[51]

After Diocletian stepped down as emperor in A.D. 305, Galerius maintained pressure on Christians in the eastern part of the empire for the next six years. The eastern Roman legions under him were first to be tested for their allegiance to the traditional religions. All Christian soldiers who refused to offer sacrifices to the gods were dismissed and later executed.

Since Lactantius had accepted the pagan rituals, he was a mere bystander of these travesties. It became very apparent to him that not to acknowledge Diocletian, the son of Jupiter, could easily be seen as disloyal or even subversive. In spite of these repugnant acts against Christians, Lactantius converted to Christianity around A.D. 303. Two years later, he was forced by Galerius to leave both his teaching position and Nicomedia. "Although he was never in the

---

50 Lactantius, *The Minor Works*, "On the Deaths of the Persecutors," trans. Mary Francis McDonald in *The Fathers of the Church*, vol. 54 (Washington: The Catholic University of America Press, 1965), 11.

51 Elizabeth DePalma Digeser, *The Making of a Christian Empire: Lactantius and Rome* (Ithaca: Cornell University Press, 2000), 2–3.

hands of torturers [during Galerius' purge], he did suffer greatly and often was destitute."[52]

Now unemployed, Lactantius devoted his energies to writing. His first book, *The Workmanship of God* (*ca.* 305), was dedicated to Demetrianus, a former student and fellow Christian. It was a tribute to God's creation of the human body, such as the eye, the nose and the tongue. Lactantius made this comment concerning human hands:

What shall I say of the hands, those ministers of reason and wisdom? *The Master Artificer* fashioned these with a plain and moderately concave surface so that whatever must be grasped can fitly occupy this surface. He terminated them in fingers in which it is difficult to settle whether appearance or utility is the greater. For their number is perfect and complete.[53]

This exposition focused on the design argument. One of the main tenets of this creationist viewpoint, as believed by Lactantius, was that all of God's works came into existence from nothing (*creatio ex nihilo*).[54] An important fact that should not be overlooked concerning Lactantius' first book is that there are absolutely no biblical references. Authors Moreschini and Norelli surmised that Lactantius "had not been a convert long and was still at home chiefly in the culture in which he had hitherto been teaching."[55]

The Divine Institutes—Lactantius' *magnum opus*—was "the most comprehensive and sophisticated Christian treatise in Latin before Augustine's *City of God*."[56] It was composed of seven chapters which can be subdivided into two sections.

The first section, composed of three chapters, was written to show that the idolatrous worship of Greek and Roman gods and the false

---

52 Lactantius, *The Divine Institutes*, "The General Introduction," trans. Mary Francis McDonald in *The Fathers of the Church*, vol. 49 (Washington: The Catholic University of America Press, 1965), xiii.

53 Lactantius, *The Minor Works*, "The Workmanship of God," 33. Italics added.

54 Lactantius, *The Divine Institutes*, 2.15. See also Anthony P. Coleman, *Lactantius the Theologian: Lactantius and the Doctrine of Providence* (Piscataway: Gorgias Press, 2017), 113–122

55 Moreschini and Norelli, *Early Christian Greek and Latin Literature*, 399.

56 Digeser, *The Making of a Christian Empire*, 11.

teachings of philosophers were both futile and irrational. The last four chapters, the second section, were penned from a Christian perspective: "True Wisdom and Religion," "Justice," "On True Worship" and "On the Blessed [Future] Life."

It was not accidental that Lactantius introduced the life and ministry of Jesus Christ in the fourth book. It became the pivotal point between the first three, marked with despair, and the last four, marked with the hope of eternal life.[57]

Lactantius presented Christianity as the only true belief system. The ultimate truth was Jesus' victory over death through his bodily resurrection. But he did not neglect to mention that Jesus' crucifixion occurred during the governorship of Pontius Pilate. He wrote,

> But those most unjust accusers began a tumult with the people whom they had aroused and demanded His crucifixion with violent cries. Then Pilate was conquered by their clamors.... But he would not deliver the sentence himself, however, and handed Him over to the Jews that they might judge Him according to their law.
>
> They led Him away, then, to be scourged with whips and before they fastened Him to the cross, they mocked Him.... Then they suspended Him between two malefactors who had been condemned for robbery, and they crucified Him.[58]

Some scholars have been rightly critical that Lactantius was too dependent upon classical sources at the expense of biblical truth. The above quotation would support this concern. This Latin scholar has incorrectly viewed Pilate as a mere pawn in the hands of the Jewish accusers. Even more egregious was his misunderstanding that the Jews were in total control of Jesus' scourging and later crucifixion.

In spite of these shortcomings, Lactantius' importance to early church history is twofold. First is his account of the life of Jesus in his fourth book, especially his death, burial and resurrection. Second is his eyewitness description of the vivid and heartrending stories of

---

57 Paul McGuckin, "The Christology of Lactantius," *Studia Patristica* 17 (1982): 814.
58 Lactantius, *The Divine Institutes*, 4.18.

the persecution endured by Christians recorded in his *On the Deaths of the Persecutors.*[59]

In A.D. 317, an elderly Lactantius was appointed by Constantine to be the Latin tutor for his son Crispus (*ca.* A.D. 300–327). Constantine had not forgotten that he and Lactantius had served together in Diocletian's court nearly two decades earlier.

Lactantius journeyed to Trier, Gaul (modern Germany), to meet up with Crispus who had been stationed there by his father. It was here that Lactantius remained until his death in A.D. 325.

Religious freedom through the Edict of Milan

Following Galerius' death in 311, much within the empire changed. The reign of terror had ended and two new emperors (*Augusti*) arose: Constantine in the west and Licinius (*ca.* A.D. 263–325) in the east.

In January 313, these two *Augusti* met in Milan, Italy. The occasion was to celebrate Licinius' marriage to Constantia, a sister of Constantine. Here the famous Edict of Milan was drawn up. This historic edict meant that Christianity was no longer illegal in the empire. With this new status, Christianity's role would not only change the religious landscape of the Roman empire but, in time, the history of the entire world. Six months later, a letter announcing this new religious policy was sent from Nicomedia to every Roman senator.

The Edict stated,

> We have long intended that the freedom of worship should not be denied but that everyone should have *the right to practice his religion as he chose.*...When under happy auspices, I, Constantine Augustus and I, Licinius Augustus had come to Milan and were discussing matters that concerned public good, among the other items of benefit to the general welfare....[60]

The italicized portion stipulated that the edict "granted freedom of worship to all religions."[61] Previously, the Roman state specified

---

59 See Lactantius, *The Minor Works*, "On the Deaths of the Persecutors," chapters 15 and 21.

60 Eusebius, *Church History*, 10.5. Italics not in the original.

61 Papandrea, *Reading the Early Church Fathers*, 180.

which gods, such as Zeus and Jupiter, were to be worshipped. No dissent was allowed.

These two Roman *Augusti* removed religious intolerance in the realm. In doing so, they made Christianity one of the state's legal religions. The intense persecution that harried Christians for the first three centuries A.D. was officially over. They now had the freedom to believe what was taught by the early church fathers—from Ignatius of Antioch to Lactantius—concerning Jesus' incarnation, death on the cross and subsequent resurrection.

CHAPTER 4

The importance of the councils of Nicaea and Constantinople

ON JULY 9, 381, the Council of Constantinopole, after almost two months of deliberation, adopted the Niceno-Constantinopolitan Creed. Three weeks later, Theodosius I (A.D. 347–395) ratified it, and the creed was sent out to all the provinces in the Roman empire as an imperial edict. The creed—undoubtedly one of the most significant documents of the early church—bore testimony that Jesus was indeed God and, during the governorship of Pontius Pilate, he was crucified, died and rose again.

During the fourth century A.D., three developments occurred that contributed to the formation of this remarkable creed: Constantine's support of Christianity, the formation of the Nicene Creed (A.D. 325) and Athanasius (*ca.* A.D. 298–373)—defender of Nicene orthodoxy.

Constantine's support of Christianity

On October 29, 312, forty-year-old Constantine entered the city of Rome and was proclaimed by the senate to be the "Liberator of the City: Founder of Peace."[1] It was this same senate that awarded Constantine, the first "professing" Christian emperor, a *triumph* (both a

---

1 This inscription dedicated to Constantine is found on the triumphal arch which stands near the Colosseum in Rome.

civil and religious ceremony) to celebrate his recent military conquests. Dressed in an all-purple, gold-embroidered toga, he was paraded through the streets of Rome. "Unlike his pagan predecessors, he declined to ascend the Capitol to perform the customary sacrifices and to give thanks to Jupiter for his victory."[2]

In the spirit of the Edict of Milan, Constantine was extremely tolerant toward other beliefs. He permitted individuals of differing faiths to serve in his administration and even in his army. He did, however, expect them to obey all new Christian legislation:

> The observance of Sunday as a holy day was prescribed for all. A law of 321 (not necessarily the first on the subject) prohibited all official business and manufacturing of artifacts on the Lord's Day.[3]

The prime motivation for the changes that Constantine implemented was to reverse the injustices committed against Christians during the nine-year Great Persecution. The church bishops "received many personal letters, honors and gifts of money from the emperor."[4] Eusebius of Caesarea wrote that all clergy "should once and for all be kept entirely free from all public duties."[5]

In his fight to reduce the influence of paganism, Constantine used the finances of the imperial treasury to build churches throughout the empire. In Rome, he authorized the construction of St. Peter's Basilica which began in 319 and was completed in 333—it was one of the most ornate and largest churches at the time.

Constantine had for some time wanted to move the capital from Rome to the eastern part of his empire. It would grant him the freedom to appoint a new senate that would be more sympathetic toward Christianity; the one in Rome still had paganistic leanings. Now, being sole emperor, he could bring to reality his dream of establishing a new eastern capital.

---

2   Timothy D. Barnes, *Constantine and Eusebius* (Cambridge: Harvard University Press, 1981), 44.

3   Barnes, *Constantine and Eusebius*, 51–52

4   Eusebius, *Church History*, 10.2.

5   Eusebius, *Church History*, 10.7.

Constantine the Great **(A.D. 272–337)**

Constantine's attitude toward Christianity has caused consternation among historians, especially as he chose an Arian, Eusebius of Nicomedia, to baptize him. There is no doubt that Constantine used Christianity to stabilize his empire and his promotion of religious freedom meant relief for Christians from the virulent persecution of past emperors. It was also Constantine who convened the Council of Nicaea in A.D. 325, a pivotal meeting of bishops from across the Roman empire.

In A.D. 326—two years after defeating his brother-in-law, Licinius—construction of *Nova Roma* (New Rome, to be known as Constantinople) began. Constantine quickly took up residence in his new capital and invited Bishop Ossius (*ca.* A.D. 256–359) of Cordoba, Spain, to be his chief advisor on religious policies. "His counsel was indispensable as he knew more Greek than the easterners knew Latin and could be trusted to speak the mind of the Roman Church in all debates."[6]

In A.D. 330, Constantinople was completed. This city was designed to be Christian in every respect.

> No paganism would be allowed in New Rome. Temples were torn down or converted into churches. New church buildings were built. Pagan statues were destroyed or altered to look like biblical characters or heroes of the faith.[7]

To equip the churches in Constantinople with Bibles, Constantine sent a letter to Eusebius of Caesarea in Palestine. This leading biblical scholar

> was to oversee the production of 50 copies of the Scriptures for Constantinople, with leather bindings, the materials to be provided by the governor together with two vehicles for their safe transport in the care of one of Eusebius' deacons.[8]

With our modern printing presses, fifty copies seems so few. But one must remember that such a request was a daunting task at the time. The entire Bible had to be meticulously written out by hand. Nevertheless, when three or four copies were completed, they were sent off to Constantinople.

---

6 Mark Edwards, "The Beginnings of Christianization," in *The Cambridge Companion to the Age of Constantine*, ed. Noel Lenski (Cambridge: Cambridge University Press, 2005), 149.

7 Papandrea, *Reading the Early Church Fathers*, 181.

8 Eusebius, *Life of Constantine*, 4.36, trans. Averil Cameron and Stuart G. Hall (Oxford: Clarendon Press, 1999), http://eclass.uth.gr/eclass/modules/document/file.php/SEAD260/Ευσέβιος,%20Life%20of%20Constantine%20(trans.%20Averil%20Cameron%20-%20Stuart%20Hall).pdf (accessed November 6, 2016).

Under the provisions of the Edict of Milan, Christianity flourished in the Roman empire. With the threat of persecution gone, freedom of thought and the exchange of ideas prevailed.

The formation of the Nicene Creed

The first major challenge that the church under Constantine faced was a theological issue of paramount importance: Was Jesus Christ truly God or was he a created being? The source from which this controversy originated was totally unexpected.

Around A.D. 313, Arius (*ca.* A.D. 256–336), a Libyan, was appointed the presbyter of a small church outside of Alexandria, Egypt. In time, this highly respected pastor began preaching that Jesus was divine but not true God "because he does not share in the Father's nature (*ousia/hypostasis*) and therefore is subordinate in terms of rank, authority and glory."[9]

Arius
(ca. A.D. 256–336)

Arius' teachings had a profound effect on the fourth-century church. He taught that Jesus was a created being and had a definite origin in time, as opposed to the trinitarian view that Jesus is co-eternal and of the same substance as the Father. Today, Jehovah Witnesses use the same biblical texts Arius used to support their assertion that Jesus is not God.

Arius had won the support and encouragement of many of the influential bishops in Palestine and Syria,[10] namely Eusebius of Caesarea and Eusebius of Nicomedia (d. A.D. 341)—two eastern theological heavyweights. It is not surprising that this heresy, called Arianism, developed in Alexandria, Egypt, "one of the greatest centers of Christian scholarship."[11] In a letter written in A.D. 318 to his bishop, Alexander (d. A.D. 328), Arius wrote:

---

9   Hubertus R. Drobner, *The Fathers of the Church: A Comprehensive Introduction*, trans. Siegfried Schatzmann (Peabody: Hendrickson, 2007), 327.

10 See Timothy D. Barnes, *Athanasius and Constantius: Theology and Politics in the Constantinian Empire* (Cambridge: Harvard University Press, 1993), 15, for a list of the supporting bishops.

11 Alistair Kee *Constantine versus Christ: The Triumph of Ideology* (London: SCM, 1982), 109.

> And God, being the cause of all things, is unbegun and alto-
> gether sole, but the Son being begotten apart from time by the
> Father, and *being created and founded before ages....* For He is
> not eternal or co-eternal or co-unoriginate with the Father.[12]

After confronting Arius who was convinced that his view concerning Jesus was totally biblical, Alexander felt that he had no other alternative but to convene a council of the Egyptian bishops. They, in turn, supported Alexander and condemned Arius of heresy.

Sensing the potential of this theological fray to disrupt the unity of the church, Constantine sent Ossius to mediate the situation. Though armed with imperial authority, Ossius failed to bring about any resolution. Learning of his emissary's failure, Constantine arranged to have bishops throughout the empire meet in Nicaea on May 20, 325. This general council, the first ecumenical gathering of the church, was to come together to resolve this pressing dilemma.

Over 300 bishops arrived at Nicaea, a city near Constantine's capital of Nicomedia (later renamed Constantinople). The overwhelming majority of the bishops, presbyters and laity were from the eastern part of the empire. Although Constantine was willing to pay the travel expenses of all the bishops throughout the empire, some declined to come because of the distance to Nicaea. The bishop of Rome, being ill and unable to attend, sent two representatives. Bishop Alexander of Alexandria came with his assistant, Athanasius.

Constantine stressed to the bishops the importance of this first ecumenical church council. The spiritual unity of the Christian church across the empire was at stake. He appointed Bishop Ossius, his trusted spiritual confidant, to preside over the daily procedures. A question most often posed by scholars is: To what extent was Constantine involved in the theological deliberations? Since no written records were kept, a definitive answer can never be known.

It should not be forgotten that these bishops were gifted, principled men. Since most were from the east, they had endured very intense persecution. "Confessors, especially those whose missing eyes and maimed ankles manifested proof of their steadfastness

---

12 "Arius' Letter to Alexander of Alexandria," *Early Church Texts*; http://www. earlychurchtexts.com/public/arius_letter_to_alexander_of_alexandria.htm (accessed November 15, 2016). Italics added.

during persecution, enjoyed enormous authority."[13] Leaders bearing these scars are rarely passive!

After three months of meetings, this assembly produced the Nicene Creed which was to be binding on all the churches across the entire empire. It read,

> We believe in one God, the Father Almighty, maker of all things visible and invisible;
>
> And in one Lord Jesus Christ, the Son of God, begotten from the Father, the only-begotten, that is, from the substance (*ousias*) of the Father, God from God and light from light; true God of true God, begotten not made, of the one substance (*homoousion*) with the Father, through whom all things came into being, things in heaven and things on earth: who for us humans and for our salvation, came down, became incarnate, becoming human, suffered, rose again on the third day, and ascended to the heavens, will come again to judge the living and the dead;
>
> And in the Holy Spirit.
>
> But, as for those who say, (1)"There was when he was not," and (2)"Before being born, he was not," and that (3) "he came into existence out of nothing" or who assert that (4) "the Son of God is of a different hypostasis" (*hypostaseōs*) or "substance" (*ousias*) or is "subject to alteration or change"—these the catholic and apostolic church anathematizes.[14]

This document was the first to articulate the foundational trinitarian and christological truths.[15] It was to become the standard upon which other creeds would follow. The triune God, acknowledging the Father, the Son and the Holy Spirit, established the framework. Since the main intent of the document was to refute Arianism, the focus was placed on the second member of the Godhead—the Lord Jesus Christ.

---

13 Barnes, *Constantine and Eusebius*, 214.

14 Drobner, *The Fathers of the Church*, 242.

15 Lewis Ayres, *Nicaea and Its Legacy: An Approach to Fourth-Century Trinitarian Theology* (Oxford: Oxford University Press, 2004), 1.

"The key phrase, however, was the line of *one substance* with the Father."[16] In the Greek, "one substance" is one word, *homoousia*; it is composed of two words: *homo* (same) and *ousia* (being or essence). The acceptance of this one word would determine the final outcome of the proceedings. Leithart has suggested that the two bishops, Ossius and Alexander, had planned beforehand to suggest to Constantine the term, *homoousia*, "as a way of weeding out Arius' allies."[17]

Contrary to Arianism, Jesus, the Son of God, was in every respect identical or in the "same substance (*homoousia*)" with the Father. As the Father was eternal, so was the Son; as the Father was omniscient, so was the Son; as the Father was omnipotent, so was the Son. In other words, the Son imaged the Father in all his divine perfection. To eliminate any misunderstanding, the bishops added the four appended anathemas. They had been slogans that Arians had used as memory aids to promote their heresy.

The Arian controversy was not the only topic on the bishops' agenda at Nicaea. Twenty canons dealt with questions related to "ecclesiastical structures (4–7, 15, 16), the dignity of the clergy (1–3, 9, 10, 17), public penance (11–14), the readmission of schismatics and heretics (8, 19) and liturgical regulations (18, 20)."[18]

The framers of this creed did not neglect the salvific plan which centred on Jesus Christ. He became incarnate, the God-man, to provide salvation to a people who were spiritually separated from God. Through his suffering and later resurrection from the dead, Jesus Christ attained for all believers eternal life.

The Council of Nicaea was undoubtedly a significant event during Constantine's reign. "As long as he lived there was no open challenge to the Nicene Creed."[19] The bishops of this general synod, with the exception of two from Libya, were in agreement with the creed. Arius' home country was Libya. Since he and the two Libyan bishops had refused to accept the decision of the synod, they were excommunicated and sent into exile. Like Athanasius of Alexandria, Arius

---

16 Gerald Bray, *Creeds, Councils and Christ* (Downers Grove: InterVarsity Press, 1984), 109. Italics added.

17 Peter J. Leithart, *Defending Constantine: The Twilight of an Empire and the Dawn of Christendom* (Downers Grove: IVP Academic, 2010), 170.

18 Drobner, *The Fathers of the Church*, 245.

19 David M. Gwynn, *Athanasius of Alexandria: Bishop, Theologian, Ascetic, Father* (Oxford: Oxford University Press, 2012), 65.

was not eligible to sign the document because he was not a bishop.

Nevertheless, the creed firmly established the primary goal of its authors by presenting Jesus Christ as Lord (*kurios*)—"God from God and light from light; true God of true God." It was he who became God incarnate in order to provide everlasting salvation for a sinful humanity, eternally damned apart from his grace.

Leithart correctly notes that the Nicene Creed was "only the first round of a theological, political and intensely personal controversy that consumed the Eastern Church through the middle decades of the fourth century."[20] A lasting resolution for these pressing issues would not come until the Niceno-Constantinopolitan Creed in A.D. 381.

Athanasius—defender of Nicene orthodoxy

Following the Council of Nicaea, Arius, the instigator, was banished to Illyricum, a province in northern Greece. It appeared, on the surface, the disaster had been averted. But, three years later, bowing to pressure from within his court, Constantine recalled Arius who, with some reservation, signed the creed. Much to the emperor's chagrin, Athanasius of Alexandria, was totally outraged that Arius—a heretic   was reinstated.

It had only been a year since Athanasius had become bishop of Alexandria following the death of Alexander. Constantine very much wanted the support of the Alexandrian bishopric as it was regarded as foremost—ecclesiastically and theologically—in the empire. Furthermore, "the title *papas* (pope), for the bishop of Alexandria some fifty years before its first attestation in Rome, accurately reflected the prestige the office held."[21]

Little is known of Athanasius' background. Born in Egypt around A.D. 298, he personally witnessed the harrowing persecution that Egyptian Christians endured. "He was taken into the bishop of Alexandria's residence as a teenager in order to prepare for a life of service to the church."[22] It was during this time that Alexander, his

---

20 Leithart, *Defending Constantine*, 171.

21 Gwynn, *Athanasius of Alexander*, 22.

22 Bradley G. Green, "Athanasius," in *Shapers of Christian Orthodoxy: Engaging with the Early and Medieval Theologians*, ed. Bradley G. Green (Downers Grove: IVP Academic, 2010), 153.

spiritual mentor, instilled in him a reverence for the Bible, the Word of the living God—a commitment that would characterize Athanasius' entire life.

Since he accompanied and assisted Alexander at Nicaea, he fully supported the Nicene Creed. Consequently, it was abhorrent to him that Constantine had the audacity to bring Arius back into church fellowship in spite of the council's condemnation of him.

For the next forty-five years (A.D. 328–373), Athanasius was bishop of Alexandria,. His tenure was interrupted five times by exile—in total, he lost seventeen years of pastoral ministry.

Athanasius' greatest fear was the impact that Arianism could have on the lives of individual believers. He understood this heresy would have a definite detrimental effect

on their salvation, on the gospel of Christ, the victory of his cross, and on their transformation by grace from darkness to light, from idolatry to co-laborers with Christ.[23]

This lifelong fight against Arianism brought Athanasius into conflict not only with the majority of eastern bishops who distrusted the Nicene Creed but also with seven emperors,[24] most of whom were pro-Arian. His most notable protagonist was Eusebius of Nicomedia, an arch-Arian supporter. His effectiveness against Athanasius surfaced when he became bishop of Constantinople, the eastern capital. It was Eusebius who baptized Constantine just before his death in A.D. 337.

Athanasius was a prolific author and focused all his writings in support of the Nicene Creed. His earliest work, *Against Paganism —On the Incarnation*,[25] revealed "the doctrinal principles that Athanasius would uphold throughout his life."[26] These foundational truths were centred on a triune God's intimate relationship with his creation, Jesus' incarnation, and the redemption and resurrection of believers.

---

23 Green, "Athanasius," in *Shapers of Christian Orthodoxy*, 167.

24 These emperors were Constantine (306–337), Constantine II (337–340), Constantius (337–361), Constants (337–350), Julian the Apostate (361–363), Valentinian (364–375) and Valens (364–375).

25 Latin: *Contra Gentes—De Incarnatione*.

26 Gwynn, *Athanasius of Alexander*, 55.

The date of this double treatise has divided scholars into two camps. Since there is absolutely no reference to Arianism, it has led some to believe that it was written before the Nicene Council of 325, while others would place it after. Most favour the later date: between A.D. 330–335.[27]

Against Paganism—On the Incarnation defended the theological position of the Nicene Creed that Jesus Christ was indeed "God from God and light from light; true God of true God."

Athanasius died in A.D. 373. Eight years after his death, the Council of Constantinople brought to fruition his lifelong goal: the recognition of the deity of God the Father, God the Son and God the Holy Spirit.

Athanasius of Alexandria (ca. A.D. 298–373)

Athanasius sent a letter to his churches in A.D. 367 in which he was the first to identify the twenty-seven books of the New Testament that are used today and considered canon. He has been called the "pillar of the church" for defence against Arianism.

The emergence of the three new Cappadocian bishops—Basil of Caesarea (A.D. 330–379), his brother Gregory of Nyssa (A.D. 335–395) and Gregory of Nazianzus (A.D. 330–389)—signaled theological support for the Nicene Creed. Each of them wrote influential works that affirmed the deity of the Holy Spirit.[28] Basil's *On the Holy Spirit* (375), according to church historian Michael Haykin, was "one of the most important books of the entire Patristic period."[29]

In May 381, the emperor Theodosius, a committed trinitarian, convened the Council of Constantinople. One-hundred-and-fifty bishops, all from the eastern part of the empire, arrived in Constantinople. After almost two months of deliberations, the council adopted

---

27 See Khaled Anatolios, *Athanasius: The Coherence of His Thought* (London: Routledge, 1998), 26, and Athanasius, *Contra Gentes and De Incarnatione*, ed. and trans. by R.W. Thomson (Oxford: Clarendon Press, 1971), xxi–xxii.

28 See Joel C. Elowsky, ed., *We Believe in the Holy Spirit* (Downers Grove: IVP Academic, 2009), xxvi–xxix. These writings were: Basil of Caesarea, *On the Holy Spirit*; Gregory of Nyssa, *On the Holy Spirit against the Macedonians*; and Gregory of Nazianzus, The Fifth Theological Oration, *On the Holy Spirit*.

29 Michael A.G. Haykin, *Rediscovering the Church Fathers: Who They Were and How They Shaped the Church* (Wheaton: Crossway, 2011), 121.

the Niceno-Constantinopolitan Creed on July 9, 381. It reads in part,

> We believe in one God, the Father, ruler, maker of heaven and of earth, and of all things both visible and invisible.
>
> And in one Lord Jesus Christ…became incarnate from the Holy Spirit and the virgin Mary, became human and *was crucified for us under Pontius Pilate* and suffered and was buried and rose up on the third day according to the Scriptures; and ascended into heaven and is seated at the Father's right hand; He is coming again with glory to judge the living and the dead; His kingdom will have no end.[30]

As with the Nicene Creed, these eastern patriarchs added six canons, each one dealing with specific spiritual concerns. Finally, as students of history, these early church fathers made reference to Pontius Pilate in the creed. They did this in order to place Jesus' death by crucifixion within a historical continuum, which now extended from the first to the fourth century.

Summary

The God of the Bible has always directed the course of history. At the precise moment in time, it was he who "sent forth His Son, born of a woman, born under the Law"[31] so that he might redeem a spiritually needy humanity. This redemption was accomplished through the crucifixion and subsequent resurrection of Jesus Christ, the God-man.

For the next four centuries, God spoke this message through the early church fathers and each heralded it to his generation. But without God's overarching control, the truth of this divine sacrifice would not have remained historically sound. The next chapters will demonstrate how Islamic scholars challenged the veracity of God's orchestrated history.

---

30 Bray, *Creeds, Councils and Christ*, 116–117. In some cases, Bray modernized the language and added new punctuation. Italics added.

31 Galatians 4:4.

CHAPTER 5

Islamic historical sources and Jesus' crucifixion

Christianity predates Islam

THE FOUNDATION OF Islam is the Qur'an. It is believed that God sent "a glorious Qur'an"[1] through Gabriel who, in turn, placed it upon Muhammad's heart. The reception of this book occurred over a period of twenty-three years (*ca.* A.D. 609–632).

Recognizing that humanity was weak and easily led away from the truth, Allah provided prophets over the centuries to give spiritual guidance for people in life's journey. "Thus, Muslims are required by the Qur'an to believe in all prophets of God, all 124,000 of them, even though the Qur'an names only twenty-one."[2]

Nevertheless, some prophets were to be favoured over others.[3] According to the Qur'an, Allah ordained five to be elite: Noah, Abraham, Moses, Jesus and Muhammad. These messengers of God were essentially of equal rank. 'Isa—the Arabic equivalent of Jesus— was viewed differently: "The Messiah, Jesus, son of Mary, was only

---

1 Sura 85:21

2 Mahmoud Ayoub, *A Muslim View of Christianity: Essays on Dialogue*, ed. Irfan A. Omar (Maryknoll: Orbis, 2007), 11. Some scholars believe there were twenty-five.

3 Sura 2:253.

a messenger of God, and his word, which he cast into Mary, and a spirit from him."[4]

A.J. Droge's rendition of humanity's rebellion states: "Then Satan caused them both [Adam and Eve] to slip [not sin] from there…. The earth is a dwelling place for you, and enjoyment (of life) for a time."[5] After Adam and Eve disobeyed, God sent them from Paradise to the earth. Islam teaches that Adam's disobedience does *not* affect the generations that followed him.

In Islamic thinking,

> that man is born sinful, or that sin is inherent in human nature, is to take the lowest possible view of human nature. No greater insult could be offered humanity than to say that a newborn child is a sinful being.[6]

Thus, the indiscretions of life are the result of one's environment whether it be delinquent parents, misguided friends or teachers.

Such indiscretions can be rectified by asking God for forgiveness and then one is to do his or her best not to commit the same offences again. Consequently, no Muslim needs a Saviour to die for his or her sins. Responsibility lies within each individual to appease Allah. "A person who purifies himself or herself by prayers, almsgiving, and other works of righteousness is a holy person."[7]

Consequently, the Qur'an asserts that it would be the greatest injustice to have Jesus, a righteous messenger, face horrible brutality and death on the cross. From an Islamic position, a merciful God had no recourse but to intervene and rescue Jesus, the Messiah.

> And for their [Jews'] saying, 'Surely we killed the Messiah, Jesus, son of Mary, the messenger of God'—*yet they did not kill him, nor did they crucify him,* but it (only) seemed like (that) to them. Surely those who differ about him are indeed in doubt about him. They have no knowledge about him, only the

---

4   Sura 4:171. There are 10 more references to Jesus in the Qur'an.

5   *The Qur'an*, trans. Droge, Sura 2:36.

6   Maulana Muhammad 'Ali, *Muhammad and Christ* (Columbus: Ahmadiyya Society for the Propogation of Islam, 1993), 30.

7   Ayoub, *A Muslim View of Christianity*, 78.

following of conjecture. *Certainly, they did not kill him.* No! God raised him up to Himself. God is mighty, wise.[8]

Radically opposed to this Islamic theology, Christianity, predating Islam by some 600 years, pictures the human condition and the person of Jesus in a much different theological light. Humanity, possessing the curse of Adam's blatant rebellion, can only find reconciliation with God through a divine substitute, namely Jesus Christ.

In the prologue of the the book of Hebrews, the author penned this portrait of Jesus:

> God, after He spoke long ago to the fathers in the prophets in many portions and in many ways, in these last days has spoken to us in His Son, whom He appointed heir of all things, through whom also He made the world. And He is the radiance of His glory and the exact representation of His nature, and upholds all things by the word of His power. When He had made purification of sins, He sat down at the right hand of the Majesty on high.[9]

"Radiance" (Greek, *apaugama*) and "exact representation of His nature" (Greek, *charaktār tās hupostaseōs*) clearly express Jesus' deity. The term "purification" (Greek, *katharismos*) is better defined by a later verse in the text. "By this will we have been sanctified through the offering of the body of Jesus Christ once for all."[10] There is absolutely no doubt that the author of Hebrews was referring to Jesus' crucifixion.

Nearly a century apart, two Muslim authors, 'Abd al-Jabbār and Muhammad 'Ata ur-Rahim, believed that the Bible's teachings were misguided and inferior to the Qur'an. Similarly, the historical Christian narrative following Jesus' ministry had also been distorted. To rectify this perversion, they authored *The Critique of Christian Origins* and *Jesus: Prophet of Islam* in order to present an Islamic interpretation of Christian history. Who were these men and what

---

8   Sura 4:157–158. Italics added.
9   Hebrews 1:1–3.
10   Hebrews 10:10.

methods did they employ to revise Christian history to make it theologically compatible with Islam?

Historical sources used in deconstructing Christianity

The Critique of Christian Origins (A.D. 995)

'Abd al-Jabbār authored *The Critique of Christian Origins* which is considered to be "the first Islamic history of Christianity… 'Abd al-Jabbār criticized Christianity not only theologically, but also on historical grounds."[11] Born in Asadābād, Iran, to a lower class family, he was later educated in Baghdad and Rey (modern-day Tehran).[12] From such humble beginnings, he rose to become the chief judge of Sharia law in Rey.

A prolific author, 'Abd al-Jabbār distinguished himself in a wide spectrum of scholarly subjects, primarily law and religion. It is estimated that "he wrote on every reputable subject—a total of over 400,000 pages!"[13] What was his incentive for writing *The Critique of Christian Origins*?

Prior to 'Abd al-Jabbār, Islamic scholars had challenged Christianity only on the level of doctrine and totally ignored its historical foundation. 'Abd al-Jabbār believed that his predecessors had failed to see that Christianity, "a human invention,"[14] should have been outrightly rejected as it was molded by Greek philosophy and pagan Roman practices.

Here in the tenth century, a Muslim scholar was connecting the celebration of Christmas with the Roman pagan festival, Saturnalia. "It was at the return of sunlight in December. They made it the birthday of Christ, adding and subtracting [things from it]."[15] According to 'Abd al-Jabbār, the founders of Christianity, especially

---

11 'Abd al-Jabbār, *The Critique of Christian Origins*, trans. and ed. Reynolds, book cover.

12 This city is also known as Rayy or Ray. "Today the ancient site of Rayy has been absorbed into the expanding metropolis of Tehran. Its ruins lie about forty-five kilometres to the south of the Iranian's capital city." Reynolds, *A Muslim Theologian in the Sectarian Milieu*, 64.

13 'Abd al-Jabbār, *The Critique of Christian Origins*, xxxv.

14 'Abd al-Jabbār, *The Critique of Christian Origins*, xix.

15 'Abd al-Jabbār, *The Critique of Christian Origins*, 3.244.

the apostle Paul, were responsible "for the suppression of the Islamic religion of Jesus and the creation of Christianity in its place."[16]

His criticism of the four Gospels was that they should have been written in Hebrew. It was this language that was spoken by Christ, Abraham and the Old Testament prophets. He reasoned that the early disciples used the Greek language so that they could easily distort the teachings of Jesus.

According to this chief justice, the greatest deception was the four Gospels' depiction of Jesus as God who became man and was later crucified. He stated that Christians incorrectly made these comments concerning Jesus. "The one equal to the Father entered the womb of the Virgin. He existed before his fathers Abraham, Israel and David."[17]

But it was the crucifixion of Jesus that garnered much of 'Abd al-Jabbār's attention.[18] He firmly believed that Jesus was not executed and that someone else other than Jesus was crucified.[19] But his most convincing evidence was that "the Cross and crucifixion were not in the original *Ingīl* [Gospels] because Jesus was not crucified [Q. 4:157]."[20]

A modern-day Muslim scholar, Mahmoud Ayoub, made a similar comment concerning the *Ingīl* and Jesus. He wrote: "Furthermore, Jesus received from God a Book which is the Gospel (*Ingīl*), confirming the Torah, revitalizing its laws, and supporting its true sanctions."[21] Both 'Abd al-Jabbār and Ayoub are relying on an Islamic tradition that the *Ingīl*, a single text, "was revealed to and proclaimed by Jesus, on the model of revelation of the Qur'an to Muhammad."[22] This text was lost or destroyed and replaced by the New Testament.

Such a tradition has no historical support. Nothing is recorded in the New Testament that Jesus received a Book from God. The

---

16 'Abd al-Jabbār, *The Critique of Christian Origins*, xix.

17 'Abd al-Jabbār, *The Critique of Christian Origins*, 1.135.

18 'Abd al-Jabbār, *The Critique of Christian Origins*, 2. 164-198; 2.396-443.

19 'Abd al-Jabbār, *The Critique of Christian Origins*, 2.463.

20 Reynolds, *A Muslim Theologian in the Sectarian Milieu*, 15. "In [the true *Injīl*] there was no mention of the crucifixion or crucifixes" ('Abd al-Jabbār, *The Critique of Christian Origins*, 3.80).

21 Ayoub, *A Muslim View Of Christianity*, 222.

22 "Glossary of technical terms in the translation" in 'Abd al-Jabbār, *The Critique of Christian Origins*, 181.

evidence available through thousands of extant manuscripts of the New Testament has convinced biblical scholars that this Islamic position is spurious.

Even though 'Abd al-Jabbār was very critical of the historical accuracy of the Bible, it should be noted that his own sources were definitely unreliable.

> Then, Pilate, the great king of the Romans, came to Herod and said to him, "It has come to me that the Jews brought up to you an Adversary of theirs who is educated and knowledgeable.... He [Jesus] was brought in to [meet] Pilate in a state of anxiety, fear and nervousness. The king calmed him and asked him about the claim of the Jews that he was the Christ. He denied having said that.... [Pilate] sent him back to Herod.[23]

Pilate is identified incorrectly here. He was definitely not the Roman emperor or king, but rather, the Roman prefect of Judea. This supposed interaction between Pilate and Herod Antipas (20 B.C.–ca. A.D. 39) and the reaction of Jesus in Pilate's presence has absolutely no historical basis. Notably, his denial of Jesus being the Messiah blatantly contravenes Islamic theology.[24]

Furthermore, it was Herod Antipas, according to 'Abd al-Jabbār, who delivered Jesus to the Jews who, in turn, were responsible for his crucifixion. It should be noted that Caiaphas, the Jewish high priest, and the Sanhedrin, the supreme court in Palestine, were never mentioned.

'Abd al-Jabbār had nothing but contempt for the apostle Paul. He writes that Paul "tore himself away from the religion of Christ and entered the religions of the Romans."[25] By doing so, Paul benefitted greatly: he was invited by the emperor to join him in his capital at Constantinople. This is also historically inaccurate. The apostle Paul went to Rome around A.D. 60, not to Constantinople—it did not become the capital in the eastern empire until A.D. 330.

---

23 'Abd al-Jabbār, *The Critique of Christian Origins*, 2.422–425.

24 See Sura 3:45. "When the angels said, 'Mary! Surely God gives you good news of a word from Him: his name is the Messiah, Jesus, son of Mary, eminent in this world and the Hereafter, and one of those brought near."

25 'Abd al-Jabbār, *The Critique of Christian Origins*, 3.158.

Even more reprehensible is 'Abd al-Jabbār's total abandonment of the *Tawrāt* or the Law of Moses. 'Abd al-Jabbār noted that Paul advised the Romans that they did not have to be circumcised. It is true that the apostle stated: "For neither is circumcision anything, nor uncircumcision, but a new creation."[26] In so far as one being reconciled with God and thus becoming a child of God, the external act of circumcision is not the determining factor but rather an internal change initiated by God.

To complete his revision of Christian history, 'Abd al-Jabbār made reference to Emperor Constantine who he deemed to be "a wicked, calculating man."[27] It was Constantine who removed the pagan worship of planets and stars and established the veneration of Jesus as God and his cross.

Arius, presbyter of a small Egyptian church, and three associates stood up against Constantine's actions. Discord erupted when they announced of Jesus: "The Word is created. The speech of God and His statement are among his creations."[28] One is not surprised that 'Abd al-Jabbār mentions Arius, as his denial of Jesus' divinity was consistent with Islamic theology.

'Abd al-Jabbār had to acknowledge that Constantine signed the Nicene Creed into law. It should be noted that 'Abd al-Jabbār did not quote the Nicene Creed but rather a modified version of the Niceno-Constantinopolitan Creed.[29] Consequently, he was aware that it advocated two major beliefs: the trinitarian view of God, specifically Jesus' deity, and his crucifixion.

'Abd al-Jabbār counteracted by stating that the creed was imposed upon the people. "Constantine continued to rule for fifty years, busy killing those who did not venerate the Cross and declare that Christ was Lord until [Christianity] became entrenched and empowered."[30] As usual 'Abd al-Jabbār's sources failed him again. Constantine did not live fifty years beyond the Nicene Creed. In actuality, he died twelve years later in A.D. 337.

---

26 Galatians 6:15.

27 'Abd al-Jabbār, *The Critique of Christian Origins*, 3.205.

28 'Abd al-Jabbār, *The Critique of Christian Origins*, 3.228.

29 'Abd al-Jabbār, *The Critique of Christian Origins*, 1.47–56.

30 'Abd al-Jabbār, *The Critique of Christian Origins*, 3.237.

By not stating his sources in his *Critique of Christian Origins*, 'Abd al-Jabbār took the opportunity to advance his Islamic agenda.

Jesus: Prophet of Islam (1977, revised 1996)

Muhammad 'Ata ur-Rahim (d. 1978) was born and raised in Hyderabad, India. Later, he attended the University of Aligarth, situated in northern India near New Delhi. Here, he received his undergraduate and graduate degrees in law and Indian history. After serving in World War II and attaining the rank of Lieutenant Colonel, he became principal of the Urdu College in Karachi, Pakistan.

Upon the death of his wife, he left Pakistan and moved to London, England, where he began his studies on the life of Jesus and Christianity. In 1977—a year before his death—he published *Jesus: Prophet of Islam*. The main theme of the book was to show that

> [Christianity] began with the belief in One God and was then corrupted and the doctrine of the Trinity came to be accepted. The result was a confusion which led men more and more away from sanity.[31]

Colonel Rahim was totally convinced that the history of Christianity, from New Testament times to the twentieth century, had been deliberately distorted. From Rahim's perspective, the only viable solution was to rewrite the history of this entire period based on the concept of a One-God unity, more commonly called Unitarianism.

Within this Unitarian worldview, Rahim examined the life of Jesus and then progressed to the fourth century focusing on Constantine and the Nicene Creed. He concluded his discussion on the Middle Ages by stating:

> Despite the tremendous power of the Roman Catholic and Protestant Churches, they could not stamp out belief in the Divine Unity. Whether it became known as Arianism, or Socianism or Unitarianism.[32]

---

31 Rahim, *Jesus: Prophet of Islam*, 9.

32 Rahim, *Jesus: Prophet of Islam*, 111.

In 1996, Ahmad Thomson,[33] a lawyer and an author himself, decided to revise, reformat and update *Jesus: Prophet of Islam*. In the preface to this revised edition, Thomson wrote that he fondly remembered times spent in the British library assisting Colonel Rahim in researching material for the original book. "These were precious days indeed, and we both learned a great deal from each other, not only about the nature and history of Christianity, but about the nature and history of Islam—and of life itself."[34] Wanting to alter as little as possible, he added only new material that he felt would enhance the original thesis.

Rahim and Thomson were totally convinced that the *Gospel of Barnabas*[35] covered "Jesus' life more extensively than any of the other Gospels."[36] To prove this point, they quoted the last ten chapters (214 to 224) from the *Gospel of Barnabas* in their entirety.[37] The main intent was to show conclusively that Judas "was so changed in speech and in face to be like Jesus that we believed him to be Jesus."[38] After which, he was taken away and crucified.

These two Muslim authors were convinced of this important idea: "Perhaps most significantly, it [the *Gospel of Barnabas*] did not contradict the account given in the Qur'an, which is the only totally reliable statement concerning this matter in existence today."[39] Oddbjørn Leirvik states, "The most widely circulated of Muslim books basing their argument on the *Gospel of Barnabas* is probably *Jesus: Prophet of Islam*."[40]

---

33 See "Ahmad," https://www.youtube.com/watch?v=tdgCuzhZPqw (November 24, 2009) for his personal testimony concerning his conversion to Islam in 1973 (accessed January 12, 2016).

34 Muhammad 'Ata ur-Rahim and Ahmad Thomson, *Jesus: Prophet of Islam*, rev. ed. (London: Ta-Ha Publishers, 1996), v.

35 In the next chapter, I will discuss whether the *Gospel of Barnabas* is a first-century or a fourteenth-century document.

36 Rahim and Thomson, *Jesus: Prophet of Islam*, 11. See also Kate Zebiri, *Muslims and Christians: Face to Face* (Oxford: Oneworld, 1997), 61.

37 Rahim and Thomson, *Jesus: Prophet of Islam*, 38–47.

38 Rahim and Thomson, *Jesus: Prophet of Islam*, 39.

39 Rahim and Thomson, *Jesus: Prophet of Islam*, 47.

40 Leirvik, *Images of Jesus Christ in Islam*, 13.

CHAPTER 6

Gospel of Barnabas—A first- or fourteenth-century document?

History of the *Gospel of Barnabas*

"GOSPEL OF BARNABAS will trigger collapse of Christianity, claims Iran,"[1] was reported in Iran's *Basij Press* in 2012. According to Turkish authorities, this Syriac[2] text of the *Gospel of Barnabas* had been confiscated from a group of smugglers in 2000. It received media attention twelve years later when the Vatican wanted to examine the leather-bound edition.

In various parts of the Muslim world, the *Gospel of Barnabas* is well known. It recalls the life of Jesus in 222 chapters. The first chapter records "the annunciation of the angel Gabriel to the Virgin Mary concerning the birth of Jesus"[3] and concludes with his final meeting with his disciples when "before their eyes the four angels carried him up to heaven."[4]

The portrayal of Jesus within the *Gospel of Barnabas* is most definitely from a Muslim perspective. Barnabas, the principal character

---

1 "Gospel of Barnabas Will Trigger Collapse of Christianity, Claims Iran," *The Christian Post* (May 25, 2012); http://www.christianpost.com/news/gospel-of-barnabas-will-trigger-collapse-of-christianity-claims-iran-75536/ (accessed January 24, 2020).

2 Syriac is a dialect of Aramaic, a language spoken in Palestine in Jesus' time.

3 *The Gospel of Barnabas* (Karachi: Fazleesons, 1974), chapter 1.

4 *Gospel of Barnabas*, chapter 221.

of the narrative, was chosen by Jesus to be one of his disciples.[5] For the next three years, he was to be Jesus' closest friend. In the biblical account in which the names of the twelve disciples are listed, there is no mention of Barnabas' name.[6]

Jesus' interaction with Satan, as depicted in the *Gospel of Barnabas*, is at odds with that of the four Gospels of the Bible. The biblical Jesus, the God-man, was always in total control when dealing with Satan. A classic example is during Jesus' temptation in the wilderness. It was Jesus who dominated as he quoted three verses from the book of Deuteronomy.[7] Satan left defeated.

Gospel of Barnabas paints a radically different relationship. Jesus, a mere man but perfect, was depicted as inferior to Satan. With an air of superiority, the master of deception replied to Jesus: "If you desire not my services neither desire I yours; for I am nobler than you, therefore, you are not worthy to serve me you are clay, while I am spirit."[8] According to the Qur'an, Satan used the identical tactic when Allah ordered him to worship Adam. His refusal was based on this premise. "I am better than he. You [Allah] created me from fire, but you created him from clay."[9]

In Luke 17:11–21, there is the incident where Jesus healed ten lepers. The one who returned and thanked him was a Samaritan. In the *Gospel of Barnabas*, it was an Ishmaelite.[10] This choice is consistent in Islamic theology, as Muslims view themselves as descendants of Ishmael. They would wholeheartedly agree with this statement from chapter 44: "Take your son, your firstborn Ishmael, and come up the mountain to sacrifice him. How is Isaac firstborn, if when Isaac was born Ishmael was seven years old?"[11] Such a position is totally contrary to the scriptural account where God said:

---

5   *Gospel of Barnabas*, chapter 14.

6   See Mark 3:16–19.

7   Matthew 4:1–11; Luke 4:1–13. The three from the book of Deuteronomy were: 8:3; 6:16 and 10:20.

8   *Gospel of Barnabas*, chapter 51. To modernize the English, see "The *Gospel of Barnabas*," Answering Christianity; http://www.answering-christianity.com/barnabas.htm (accessed February 3, 2018).

9   Sura 7.12. Satan could make this statement as he was considered to be a *jinn*—a supernatural creature.

10   *Gospel of Barnabas*, chapter 19.

11   *Gospel of Barnabas*, chapter 44.

Take now your son, your only son, whom you love, Isaac, and go to the land of Moriah, and offer him there as a burnt offering on one of the mountains of which I will tell you.[12]

The history of this controversial document goes back to the time of John Toland (1670–1722), an Enlightenment and deistic philosopher. His first book, *Christianity not Mysterious* (1696), was a rationalistic approach to Christianity. In 1709, he received a copy of the *Gospel of Barnabas* from John Frederic Cramer (d. 1715), then residing in Amsterdam, who was an advisor to the king of Prussia.[13]

Nine years later in *Nazarenus, or Jewish, Gentile and Mahometan Christianity* (1718), Toland devoted an entire chapter to the *Gospel of Barnabas*. In the preface, he stated: "It is a Muslim Gospel never before publicly made known among Christians."[14] Toland believed the *Gospel of Barnabas* was "closer to original Jewish Christianity than the biblical Gospels."[15] Its presentation of Jesus was totally in harmony with the teachings of Islam.

As a deist, Toland had absolutely no confidence in the Bible—especially its description of Jesus as God. He realized that he could cast doubt on the validity of the biblical Gospels by affirming the *Gospel of Barnabas*. Consistent with his anti-Christian bias, Toland penned these words in his conclusion to *Nazarenus, or Jewish, Gentile and Mahometan Christianity*: "What the Muslims

John Toland
(1670–1722)

Born in Ireland, John Toland was educated at the universities of Glasgow, Edinburgh, Leiden (Holland) and Oxford. He became a rationalist philosopher and strongly doubted the veracity of the Bible. He promoted the *Gospel of Barnabas* as a reliable document.

---

12 Genesis 22:2.

13 John Toland, *Nazarenus, or, Jewish, Gentile, and Mahometan Christianity* (1718), 5:14-15; https://books.google.ca/books?id=PQ5PAAAAcAAJ&printsec=frontcover&source=gbs_ge_summary_r&cad=o#v=onepage&q&f=false (accessed January 30, 2017).

14 Toland, *Nazarenus, or, Jewish, Gentile, and Mahometan Christianity*, ii.

15 Leirvik, *Images of Jesus Christ in Islam*, 136.

believe concerning Christ and his doctrine…they are as old as the time of the Apostles…yet some of those things are founded on another Gospel, anciently known, and still in some manner existing, attributed to Barnabas."[16]

George Sale (1697–1736), a contemporary of Toland, had a different evaluation of "this so-called Gospel." Two years prior to his death in 1734, he completed the translation of the Qur'an into English. For the next 150 years, it remained the preferred version. In his preliminary discourse where he outlines his sources, he made mention of the *Gospel of Barnabas*. He noted that this work resembled the four canonical ones but added this critical assessment:

> From the design of the whole, and the frequent interpolations of stories and passages wherein Muhammad is spoken of and foretold by name, as a messenger of God, and the great prophet who was to perfect the dispensation of Jesus, it appears to be *a barefaced forgery*.[17]

In 1907, Anglican missionaries to Cairo, Lonsdale (1866–1945) and Laura (1865–1962) Ragg edited and translated the *Gospel of Barnabas* from Italian into English. They devoted four years of their lives to accomplish this momentous feat. Their seventy-page introduction provided a wealth of important information concerning the history of the manuscripts of *Barnabas*.

These two British scholars examined "the Subject Matter of Barnabas"[18] from both a biblical and qur'anic perspective. Nevertheless, they were of the opinion that "the Italian manuscript was probably a deliberate forgery of the latter half of the sixteenth century."[19]

In 1908 Rashid Rida (1865–1935), an Islamic reformer, translated the *Gospel of Barnabas* into Arabic. Muslim interest in the English version skyrocketed; it was printed in such countries as Egypt,

---

16 Toland, *Nazarenus, or, Jewish, Gentile, and Mahometan Christianity*, 84–85.

17 George Sale, *A Comprehensive Commentary on the Qur'an: Comprising Sale's Translation and Preliminary Discourse*, ed. E.M. Wherry (Boston: Houghton, Mifflin and Company, 1882), 11. Italics not in the original.

18 "Introduction," *The Gospel of Barnabas*, ed. and trans. Lonsdale and Laura Ragg (Oxford: Clarendon Press, 1907), xxvii-xxv; https://archive.org/stream/thegospelofbarnoounknuoft#page/n2/mode/1up (accessed March 9, 2020)

19 David Sox, *The Gospel of Barnabas* (London: George Allen and Unwin, 1984), 28.

Pakistan and India. Without exception, the Raggs' introduction was removed.

Jack McNeilus in his article, "What Missiologists should know about the *Gospel of Barnabas*," made some very disparaging comments about these Muslim printers for their reprinting of the Raggs' rendering without their permission: "The pirated work can be vaguely comprehended by understanding Islamic culture; a Muslim may lie to protect his religion from dishonor."[20]

In 1911, Samuel Zwemer (1867–1952) founded and edited the journal *The Moslem World*. For the next thirty-seven years, Zwemer, known as "the Apostle to Islam,"[21] published articles about evangelistic efforts in the Islamic world. In 1923, he wrote an article about the *Gospel of Barnabas*. One interesting comment he made was this "Gospel"—allegedly written in the first century A.D.—had numerous references to the Qur'an—a document composed 700 years later. To him, the *Gospel of Barnabas* was nothing but "a flagrant forgery."[22]

Supporters for a first-century document

The popularity of the *Gospel of Barnabas* has prompted many Muslims, when dialoguing with Christians, to ask:

Why has the Christian world hidden the *Gospel of Barnabas*? This illuminating book proves that Jesus was a true Prophet of Islam, proving that he never claimed to be the Son of God and that he predicted the coming of the Prophet by name.[23]

The leading modern-day proponent for the *Gospel of Barnabas* would be the late Mohammad 'Ata ur-Rahim. He co-ordinated the

---

20 Jack McNeilus, "What Missiologists Should Know about the Gospel of Barnabas," *Journal of Adventist Mission Studies*, Vol. 8, No. 2 (2012): 96; http://digitalcommons.andrews.edu/cgi/viewcontent.cgi?article=1211&context=jams (accessed November 9, 2017).

21 Alan Neely, "Zwemer, Samuel Marinus," in *Biographical Dictionary of Christian Missions*, ed. Gerald H. Anderson (New York: Macmillan Reference USA, 1998), 763; http://www.bu.edu/missiology/missionary-biography/w-x-y-z/zwemer-samuel-marinus-1867-1952/ (accessed November 7, 2017).

22 Samuel Zwemer, "The Gospel of Barnabas," *The Moslem World* 13 (1923): 278.

23 "The Gospel of Barnabas," *Arabic Bible Outreach Ministry* (2016); http://www.arabicbible.com/for-muslims/barnabas-gospel/180-gospel-rejected-by-christianity-why/1573-the-gospel-of-barnabas.html (accessed January 31, 2017).

1974 publication of the *Gospel of Barnabas* with the Raggs' English translation but, as expected, removed the introduction. Surely, he was aware of the Raggs' evaluation of this book, which they deemed to be written in "a medieval environment; in the atmosphere of the thirteenth century."[24]

Nevertheless, Rahim prefaced the book with such subheadings as "Life and Message of Barnabas," "Mohammad and Jesus in the Bible" and finally, "Unitarianism in the Bible."[25] The material in this preface became foundational for his book, *Jesus: Prophet of Islam* (1977). Within a year and a half after the *Gospel of Barnabas* was released, there were 18,000 copies in circulation.

Colonel Rahim was convinced the traditional understanding of the history of Christianity since the first century was inaccurate and totally deceptive. In order to rectify these "historical fallacies," he authored *Jesus: Prophet of Islam*, where he presented what he considered to be the only valid interpretative tool: the perspective of a One-God unity or Unitarianism. In this reinterpretation of western Christian history, Rahim was entirely dependent on the *Gospel of Barnabas*. It was this first-century account of Jesus that Rahim believed provided a historically sound foundation.

According to Rahim, the author of the *Gospel of Barnabas* was the only disciple who was a constant follower of Jesus during his three-year ministry. Hence, "he had direct experience and knowledge of Jesus' teaching, unlike the authors of the four accepted Gospels."[26] It was he who, in the prologue of his gospel, could write: "Barnabas, apostle of Jesus of Nazarene, called Christ, to all them that dwell upon the earth desiring peace and consolation."[27]

The unreliability of the four canonical Gospels of the New Testament was a major theme in Rahim's work. Since the originals had been destroyed, "People can only speculate as to how much of the Gospel was changed or altered during these transitions from one language to another."[28] Thus, the *Gospel of Barnabas* was the only

---

24 *The Gospel of Barnabas*, ed. and trans. Ragg and Ragg, xxxvi; https://archive.org/stream/thegospelofbarnoounknuoft#page/n2/mode/1up (accessed February 7, 2017).

25 *Gospel of Barnabas*, v–xxviii.

26 Rahim, *Jesus: Prophet of Islam*, 39.

27 *Gospel of Barnabas*, prologue.

28 Rahim, *Jesus: Prophet of Islam*, 44.

reliable historical source upon which one can build a valid interpretation of the history of Western Christianity.

Ahmad Thomson, wanting to promote his mentor's version of Western Christianity, revised and updated *Jesus: Prophet of Islam* in 1996. On January 17, 2017, he wrote a lengthy two-part article, "The Gospel of Barnabas," in which he perpetuated a number of historical errors. One in particular is that he says the second-century church father Irenaeus "quoted extensively from the *Gospel of Barnabas* in support of his views."[29] Cyril Glassé (1944–), a Muslim intellectual and author of *The New Encyclopedia of Islam*, took issue with Thomson's assertion.

First, he stated that the *Gospel of Barnabas* was "an 'apocryphal' account of the life of Jesus (not to be confused with the 'Epistle of Barnabas'."[30] It is highly significant that Glassé drew a distinction between the *Gospel of Barnabas* and the Epistle of Barnabas.[31] This epistle was well known by Irenaeus and other church fathers. But, by the fourth century, it was no longer considered canonical and consequently fell into disuse. Ahmad Thomson's failure to see the difference between these two sources is most definitely a strike against his credibility and scholarship.

Lastly, M. Yusseff, a Muslim scholar, introduced an entirely new approach in showing that the *Gospel of Barnabas* was written in the first century A.D.. He compared the similarities between the scrolls found in the Qumran (1947–1956) with the *Gospel of Barnabas*. By doing so, he has argued that "in antiquity and authenticity, no other gospel can come close to the *Gospel of Barnabas*."[32]

---

29 Ahmad Thomson, "The Gospel of Barnabas," *Tell Me about Islam*, 2 parts (2017): http://www.tellmeaboutislam.com/the-gospel-of-barnabas.html (accessed December 4, 2017), 1.2.

30 "Barnabas, the Gospel," in Cyril Glassé, *The New Encyclopedia of Islam*, 4th ed. (Lanham: Rowman & Littlefield, 2013), 90. Within the same article he states: "There is no question that it [*Gospel of Barnabas*] is of medieval origin."

31 It is usually thought that this document was written in Alexandria, Egypt, between A.D. 70–132. Its theme can be summarized in two questions: (1) How should Christians interpret the Hebrew Scriptures? (2) What is the nature of the relationship between Christianity and Judaism after the Fall of Jerusalem in A.D. 70? See Glenn Davis, "Epistle of Barnabas," *The Development of the Canon of the New Testament* (1997–2010); http://www.ntcanon.org/Epistle_of_Barnabas.shtml (accessed February 7, 2017).

32 M.A. Yusseff, *The Dead Sea Scrolls, The Gospel of Barnabas and the New Testament* (Indianapolis: American Trust, 1990), 5.

Yusseff was convinced that, had Lonsdale and Laura Ragg been aware of the Dead Sea Scrolls four decades earlier, they possibly would not have deemed the *Gospel of Barnabas* as spurious. This American scholar noted that the Essenes wanted to separate themselves from the worldliness and godlessness of the Jewish society of their day, so they moved to the desert area by the Dead Sea. Here, they lived a monastic life, devoting themselves to the copying of the Hebrew scriptures and writing commentaries on books of the Bible.

Yusseff saw a commonality between the beliefs espoused by the Essenes and the author of the *Gospel of Barnabas*. Each saw themselves as followers of the Abrahamic faith and bound to a meticulous observance of Mosaic Law.

The Essenes could be described as an "apocalyptic sect of Judaism."[33] They believed the Messiah was yet to come; he would be someone like King David, a kingly figure, and like Aaron, a priestly one. For Yusseff, this belief was identical to the one predicted by Jesus in the *Gospel of Barnabas*. When talking to the woman of Samaria, "Barnabas" had Jesus say: "I am indeed sent to the house of Israel as a prophet of salvation; but after me shall come the Messiah sent of God to all the world."[34]

Within the academic community, there is little support that "Jesus, himself, or maybe John the Baptist were members of this [Essene] group. And that cannot be proven at all."[35] Unheard of until its translation by the Raggs in 1907, the *Gospel of Barnabas* has found a reading audience primarily in the Middle East. It is estimated that by 2016 there were over 100,000 copies in circulation.[36]

Supporters for a fourteenth-century document

Mathias Zahniser, an authority in both Christian and Islamic theology, has been forthright in stating that the *Gospel of Barnabas* was "a medieval forgery."[37] In his book *The Mission and Death of Jesus in*

---

33 L. Michael White, "The Essenes and the Dead Sea Scrolls: What does the discovery of these scrolls reveal about first century Judaism and the roots of Christianity?" PBS *Frontline* (1998); http://www.pbs.org/wgbh/pages/frontline/shows/religion/portrait/essenes.html (accessed November 11, 2017).

34 *Gospel of Barnabas*, chapter 82.

35 White, "The Essenes and the Dead Sea Scrolls."

36 "The Gospel of Barnabas," *Arabic Bible Outreach Ministry*, 1.

37 Zahniser, *The Mission and Death of Jesus in Islam and Christianity*, 86.

Islam and Christianity, he outlines the geographical, historical and Islamic theological inaccuracies. His work clearly illustrates that both Rahim and Thomson had little concern for the veracity of the information they presented.

Geographical errors

The author of the *Gospel of Barnabas* lacked a proper understanding of the geography of Palestine. He wrote: "Jesus went to the sea of Galilee, and having embarked in a ship *sailed to his city of Nazareth.*"[38] The city of Nazareth is 64 kilometres (40 miles) *inland* from the Sea of Galilee.

The author of the *Gospel of Barnabas* makes the same mistake when he has Jesus and his disciples embark on a boat to go to Jerusalem.[39] Furthermore, he has Jesus taking excursions to Damascus, Syria[40] and to Mount Sinai.[41] Is it any wonder that Lonsdale Ragg and his wife, the first translators of the *Gospel of Barnabas,* noted: "Evidently he [Barnabas] possessed no first-hand knowledge of Palestine, still less of Palestine in the first century of our era."[42]

Historical errors

Historian anachronisms plague this book. For example, "Barnabas" wrote:

> There reigned at that time in Judaea Herod, by decree of Caesar Augustus, and Pilate was governor in the priesthood of Annas and Caiaphas.[43]

This passage shows that at the time of Jesus' birth (*ca.* 5 or 6 B.C.), "Barnabas" had Herod the Great being contemporaneous with Annas, Caiaphas and Pilate. Such a statement is a historical impossibility. Annas did not become high priest until A.D. 6 and Caiaphas,

---

38　*Gospel of Barnabas,* chapter 20. Italics added.

39　*Gospel of Barnabas,* chapters 151–152.

40　*Gospel of Barnabas,* chapters 139 and 143

41　*Gospel of Barnabas,* chapter 92. It is recorded: "At this time we with Jesus, by the word of the holy angel, were gone to Mount Sinai. And there Jesus with his disciples kept for Forty days."

42　"Introduction," *The Gospel of Barnabas,* ed. Ragg and Ragg, xxi.

43　*Gospel of Barnabas,* chapter 3. See also chapter 93 for identical dating problems.

his son-in-law, not until A.D. 18. Even more remote was Pilate who did not become governor of Judea until A.D. 26.

Credible historians have placed the writing of the *Gospel of Barnabas* in the fourteenth century. The author's reference to nine heavens[44] is similar to that in *Dante's Inferno* (1314). Notably, the Qur'an has seven.[45] Lonsdale Ragg was not only an outstanding linguist but also was known as an expert on the writings of Dante (1265–1321). In commenting on the view that "Barnabas" had concerning hell in chapters 59 and 60, Ragg wrote:

> the description of the pains and cries of the damned in the gospel [were] "strongly reminiscent" of the Italian poet; the picture of hell in Barnabas was remarkably similar to that in the master's *Inferno*.[46]

It has been speculated that "Barnabas" was possibly a Roman Catholic monk or priest who had converted to Islam. He made two glaring anachronisms that definitively indicate that he lived during the fourteenth century.

> "If man could change dung into gold and clay into sugar, what would he do?" Then, Jesus being silent, the disciples answered: "No one would exercise himself in any way other than in making gold and sugar."[47]

In his scholarly article, Jan Joosten feels that the reference to sugar definitively dates the book within the medieval period. Refined sugar was unknown to people in Jesus' day. As Joosten correctly states: "In the fourteenth century, imported sugar was an expensive rarity in Europe."[48]

---

44 *Gospel of Barnabas*, chapter 178.

45 Sura 2:29.

46 D. Sox, The *Gospel of Barnabas* (London: George Allen and Unwin, 1984), 31.

47 *Gospel of Barnabas*, chapter 119.

48 Jan Joosten, "The Date and Provenance of the 'Gospel of Barnabas,'" *Journal of Theological Studies* 61 (April 2010): 210–221. Joosten mentions: "Sugar was invented in India and came to the West through the Arab world. All through the Middle Ages, its production remained a monopoly of the Arabs."

The other anachronism occurred when "Barnabas" mentions that soldiers rolled "casks of wood when they were washed to refill them with wine."[49] In the ancient world, wine was carried in animal skins not wooden casks.

One further important historical consideration is that 'Abd al-Jābbar makes no mention of the *Gospel of Barnabas*. There are two possible explanations for this tenth-century author ignoring this work. One could be that he was unaware of it. This seems highly unlikely, as he had the four canonical Gospels in his possession. The other is that the *Gospel of Barnabas* was not written until at least three centuries later—as scholars have contended for some time.

Lack of knowledge of Islamic theology

The author of the *Gospel of Barnabas* has an extensive knowledge of both the Old and New Testaments. He refers to

> twenty-two of the thirty-nine books of the Hebrew Bible…. showing preference to the Psalms and Isaiah…. As far as the New Testament is concerned, references are made in some way to nineteen of the twenty-seven canonical books.[50]

In tracing the life of Jesus from his virgin birth to his ascension to heaven, "Barnabas" followed the pattern of the canonical Gospels.

Of his familiarity with the Bible, there seems little doubt. But, on the other hand, his knowledge of Islam is somewhat limited. In Jesus' dialogue with the woman of Samaria, the author of the *Gospel of Barnabas* contradicted a major Islamic teaching:

> Said the woman: "O Lord, perhaps you are the Messiah."
>
> Jesus answered: "I am indeed sent to the House of Israel as a prophet of salvation; but after me shall come the Messiah, sent of God to all the world.[51]

This denial of Jesus being the Messiah is totally at odds with the Qur'an. It states:

---

49 *Gospel of Barnabas*, chapter 152.
50 Zahniser, *The Mission and Death of Jesus in Islam and Christianity*, 89.
51 *Gospel of Barnabas*, chapter 82. See also chapters 70, 96 and 198.

> When the angels said, "Mary! Surely God gives you good news
> of a word from Him: his name is the Messiah, Jesus, son of
> Mary, eminent in this world and the Hereafter, and one of those
> brought near."[52]

"Barnabas" seems to place Jesus as the forerunner of Muhammad. There is no mention of John the Baptist.

Shabir Ally, president of the Islamic Centre in Toronto, Canada, has expressed his concern about the veracity of the *Gospel of Barnabas*. During an interview, he said, "I hesitate to use it as an authentic account because of the way that Muslims authenticate matters by having a chain of authority to relate to a historical event."[53] Since this document suddenly appeared during the Middle Ages and does not having a reliable chain of authority, Ally has discounted the book as non-historical.

Another attempt to present the Islamicization of the Bible and Western Christian history was recorded in *The Mysteries of Jesus: A Muslim Study of the Origins and Doctrines of the Christian Church* by Ruqaiyyah Maqsood. (Prior to her conversion to Islam, she had written six books on Christianity and has maintained the same zeal as a Muslim.) She devoted the entire appendix of her book to the *Gospel of Barnabas*, as it very much resonated with her Islamic beliefs. She regarded the work as "a beautiful and interesting document, written with considerable skill, and [having] some very interesting phrases and variant teachings."[54]

John Gilchrist, a tireless South African Christian apologist, took a radically different approach in evaluating the historical worth of the *Gospel of Barnabas*. In his excellent article, "Origins and Sources of the *Gospel of Barnabas*," he did not mince any words about this fourteenth-century document:

> A general study of its contents and authorship shows that it is
> a poor attempt to forge a life of Jesus consonant with the profile

---

52 Sura 3:45. Other references are 4:171; 5:72–73.

53 Safiyyah Ally, host, "*Gospel of Barnabas*, Is it Real?—Dr. Shabir Ally," *Let the Quran Speak* (August 6, 2014); https://www.youtube.com/watch?v=KALwiuy5-5I (accessed January 24, 2020).

54 Ruqaiyyah Waris Maqsood, *The Mysteries of Jesus: A Muslim Study of the Origins and Doctrines of the Christian Church* (Oxford: Sakina, 2000), 228.

of Jesus in the Qur'an and Islamic tradition. The Muslim world will do well to reject this book as *a clear forgery*—for that is what it unmistakably proves to be.[55]

---

55 John Gilchrist, "Origins and Sources of the Gospel of Barnabas," *Facing the Muslim Challenge: A Handbook of Christian-Muslim Apologetics* (1999); http://www.bible.ca/Islam/library/Gilchrist/barnabas/html (accessed April 20, 2017). Italics added.

CHAPTER 7

The deconstruction of the Islamic interpretation of the rise of Christianity

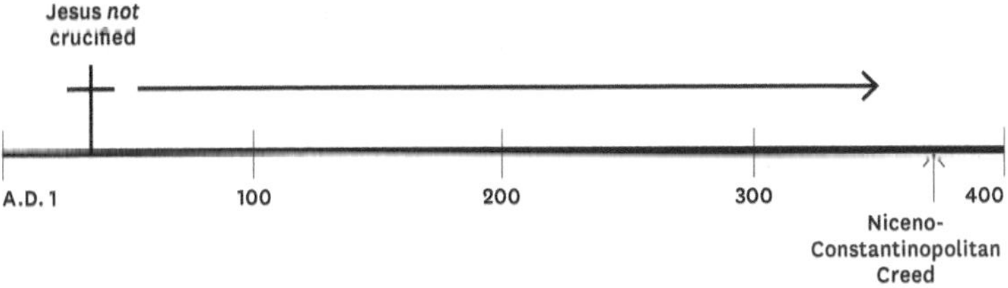

Deconstruction of *Jesus: Prophet of Islam*

JESUS: PROPHET OF ISLAM has become recognized as the most comprehensive Muslim interpretation of Christian history. The authors, Muhammad 'Ata ur-Rahim and Ahmad Thomson, either ignored or distorted the primary sources in order to present the Islamic theological position that Jesus did not die on the cross.

Even though the major theme of *Jesus: Prophet of Islam* was the impact of Unitarianism upon Church history from the first to the twentieth century, only the first four chapters will be studied as they specifically relate to our historical period of A.D. 33–381.

The Qur'an, written between A.D. 609 and 632, taught that Jesus was not God and that he did not die by crucifixion based upon one verse, Sura 4:157. Committed to the Qur'anic teachings, Rahim and

Thomson took it upon themselves to revise the history of the first four centuries to align them with Islamic theology.

They were not bound by any objective primary sources; consequently, driven by their Islamic bias, subjectivity permitted Rahim and Thomson to fabricate narratives which had no historical basis. Numerous errors can be found in *Jesus: Prophet of Islam*. I have chosen to concentrate on four areas: the *Gospel of Barnabas*, the apostle Paul's conversion and his relationship to Mosaic law, Irenaeus and the Nicene Creed.

It will become very obvious that Rahim's and Thomson's first concern was to make Christian history conform to Islamic ideology at all costs. They had no regard for historical truth or accuracy. Of the four areas mentioned above, there are two that should not be overlooked: Popea and her influence on the conversion of the apostle Paul and the miraculous selection of the four Gospels during the Council of Nicaea.

The process of deconstructing Rahim's and Thomson's *Jesus: Prophet of Islam* must begin by examining their foundational document—the *Gospel of Barnabas*.

Jesus: Prophet of Islam

Authors Muhammad 'Ata ur-Rahim's and Ahmad Thomson's efforts to make Christian history conform to Islamic idealogy was encapsulated in this book and relied significantly on the *Gospel of Barnabas*.

Gospel of Barnabas—the fictitious "Gospel"

Jesus: Prophet of Islam was totally based upon the premise that the *Gospel of Barnabas* was written in the first century A.D. by an author named "Barnabas." In 2017, Ahmad Thomson stated: "Barnabas therefore had a direct experience and knowledge of Jesus' teaching, unlike all the authors of the four officially accepted Gospels."[1]

---

1   Thomson, "The Gospel of Barnabas," *Tell Me about Islam*, 1.2.

The historicity of the *Gospel of Barnabas* for these two authors was crucial. In the balance was the acceptance of Jesus' life and his message.

> If it is false, then the Gospel of Barnabas' message about who 'Isa [Islamic name for Jesus] is becomes untrustworthy. Moreover, if the Gospel of Barnabas is false, then without a doubt, Iblis [the name for the devil in the Qur'an] is certainly deceiving Islam about 'Isa. *If the Gospel of Barnabas is a forgery, then it discredits Islam, the Qur'an, and their proponents.*[2]

Louay Fatoohi, a prolific author, and an ardent advocate of Islam believes that the *Gospel of Barnabas* is "an aprocryphal document."[3] But he admits that "non-Muslim scholars in general consider the work to be late and a forgery."[4]

Interestingly, Thomson also alluded to the Christian claims made regarding the *Gospel of Barnabas* being a forgery by some medieval renegade Muslims. These detractors' comments, he felt, "are simply vain attempts to dismiss a Gospel that strikes at the heart of contemporary Christian Christology."[5] What is more surprising is that Thomson made absolutely no attempt to discount the historical, geographical or theological inaccuracies leveled against the "Gospel."

Support for *Jesus: Prophet of Islam* has consistently come from Islamic quarters as it unquestioningly advocates the Qur'anic teaching that Jesus was not crucified. In the book, Rahim and Thomson quote the last ten chapters (214 to 224) of the *Gospel of Barnabas*.[6] Their main intent was to show conclusively that Judas "was so changed in speech and in face to be like Jesus that we believed him to be Jesus."[7] After which, Judas was taken away and crucified. Not

---

2   McNeilus, "What Missiologists Should Know about the Gospel of Barnabas," 96. Italics added.

3   Louay Fatoohi, *The Mystery of the Crucifixion: The Attempt to Kill Jesus in the Qur'an, the New Testament, and Historical Sources* (Birmingham: Luna Plena, 2008), 112.

4   Fatoohi, *The Mystery of the Crucifixion*, 113–114.

5   Thomson, "The Gospel of Barnabas," *Tell me about Islam*, 1.2.

6   Rahim and Thomson, *Jesus: Prophet of Islam*, 38–47.

7   Rahim and Thomson, *Jesus: Prophet of Islam*, 39.

one of the early church fathers during the first four centuries ever recorded that Judas died in Jesus' place. Undoubtedly, the *Gospel of Barnabas* must be deemed fictitious.

Paul's conversion

In his letter to the church at Philippi, Paul gave a brief description of his spiritual background.[8] Born in a highly orthodox Jewish family, Saul (later known as Paul) understood the importance of Mosaic law—all his life revolved around it. To further understand the intricacies of the law, he studied under the renowned Pharisaic teacher Gamaliel. Saul, a brilliant and dedicated student, advanced "in Judaism beyond many of my contemporaries among my countrymen, being more extremely zealous for my ancestral traditions."[9]

Not being able to fathom how some of his fellow Jews could forsake Judaism to become Christians, Saul aggressively persecuted them. Knowing that some of the followers of the Way had sought refuge in Damascus, armed with letters from the high priest, he was determined to bring them back to Jerusalem. En route to the Syrian capital, this crusading zealot experienced God's intervention into his life. Paul later wrote:

> But when God, who had set me apart *even* from my mother's womb and called me through His grace, was pleased [*eudokēsen*][10] to reveal His Son in me so that I might preach Him among the Gentiles....[11]

Through this supernatural encounter with the Lord Jesus Christ, Paul came to realize that righteousness could not be attained by keeping the law of Moses. A righteousness that was pleasing to a holy God was granted to Paul when he placed his faith in Jesus Christ who paid the penalty for his sins on the cross.

---

8 Philippians 3:4–6.

9 Galatians 1:14.

10 *Eudokēsen* comes from *eudokein*, meaning "to seem good or pleasing." But it could also be rendered "to resolve or determine." These possible meanings are more forceful. Then, Paul's conversion could be understood as an act which was totally under God's timing and direction.

11 Galatians 1:15–16. Italics in the original.

The description of Paul's conversion is drastically different in *Jesus: Prophet of Islam*. Not relying on any credible objective sources including the Bible, Rahim and Thomson used their fertile imaginations to concoct a bizarre explanation of why Saul, a dedicated Jew, adopted Christianity. They speculated that Saul had become infatuated with a vivacious woman named Popea. This daughter of the Jewish high priest rejected Saul's marriage proposal. Instead, she went to Rome as an actress.

> Starting on the stage, she climbed step by step until she reached Nero's bed. Ultimately she married him and so became Empress of the Roman Empire.[12]

According to these two Muslim authors, "Paul therefore had a good reason to resent both the Jews and the Romans. Paul's conversion coincided with his being rejected by Popea."[13] Being so emotionally disillusioned, he became spiritually vulnerable; it was during this state of vulnerability that he had a vision in which he both saw and heard Jesus of Nazareth.

Rahim and Thomson have suggested that Paul's spiritual crisis impacted another crucial area of his life: he was changed from being "one of the greatest supporters of the Jewish Law to one of its greatest enemies."[14]

The role of the Mosaic law misunderstood

To substantiate Paul's change in attitude toward the Mosaic law, the authors of *Jesus: Prophet of Islam* quote Galatians 3:25: "Now that faith has come, we are no longer under the supervision of the law."[15] They not only misquoted the verse but they also showed that they had absolutely no understanding of its cultural setting. Without this knowledge, the intent of the verse is lost.

Placed in its proper scriptural context, it reads as follows:

---

12 Rahim and Thomson, *Jesus: Prophet of Islam*, 56.
13 Rahim and Thomson, *Jesus: Prophet of Islam*, 56.
14 Rahim and Thomson, *Jesus: Prophet of Islam*, 56.
15 Rahim and Thomson, *Jesus: Prophet of Islam*, 70.

> Therefore the Law has become our tutor *to lead us* [*paidagōgos*]
> to Christ, so that we may be justified by faith. But now that
> faith has come, we are no longer under a tutor.[16]

The Greek words *paidagōgos nuōn*[17] translate as "our tutor to lead us." Inherent within the term *paidagōgos* is an ancient Roman custom that set forth the stages a son from a wealthy family goes through before reaching manhood. The apostle Paul used this analogy to illustrate the role the law played within the life of a believer.

A Roman father would choose a *paidagōgos*, usually a Greek slave, to care for his son from the age of six to twelve years. Staying with the boy day and night, the *paidagōgos* "protected his charge and prevented him from experiencing physical and moral harm and educated him in all manners of conduct and speech."[18]

When the boy reached the age of twelve, his father would have to decide whether his son was mature enough to take on the responsibility of manhood. If the father was convinced his son had reached proper maturity, there would be a ceremony in which his son would publicly be declared a man. In this new role, the son became the master while his *paidagōgos* became his slave.

Using this metaphor, Paul is saying the Mosaic law is the *paidagōgos*. Since all individuals are endowed with a conscience from conception onward, they have the moral law inscribed on their hearts.[19] Like the *paidagōgos*, it not only constantly monitors their behaviour but also alerts them to the reality that they have broken the demands of this code.

"For through the Law I died to the Law, so that I might live to God."[20] Since the law has condemned all to be law-breakers, it also points them to Christ, who can provide them with the only way to become justified before a holy and righteous God. For the apostle Paul, the Mosaic law was never abandoned. Rather, followers of Christ possess the One who resides within them to fulfil the demands of the law.

---

16 Galatians 3:24–25. Italics in the original.

17 *Paidagōgos* is the combination of *pais* (boy) and *agōgos* (a leader).

18 Williams, *Paul's Metaphors*, 62.

19 Romans 2:15.

20 Galatians 2:19.

A Greek teacher (left) instructs a Roman boy while his *paidagōgos* watches

Contrary to Rahim's and Thomson's understanding, the apostle Paul always had a positive attitude toward the Mosaic law. He wrote: "So then, the Law is holy, and the commandment is holy and righteous and good."[21]

Paul realized there was nothing imperfect with God's law. The problem was not the law but with men and women who continually disobeyed it. The Scriptures have confirmed this reality: "For all have sinned and fall short of the glory [perfection] of God."[22] Thus, as sinners, humanity has viewed the law as a curse because, by violating it, people are condemned and will be eternally separated from God.

Both Jesus and Paul realized there was only one solution. Jesus used the term, "born again" or "born from above."[23] Having the same intent, the apostle declared that every person must become "a new creation."[24] This change of identity is accomplished through Jesus' sacrificial death on the cross and his subsequent resurrection from the dead.

---

21 Romans 7:12.
22 Romans 3:23.
23 John 3:3.
24 Galatians 6:15.

Paul's relationship with the Lord Jesus Christ settled the question surrounding the law of Moses once and for all. Righteousness once sought by keeping the law was replaced by a righteousness gained through faith in Jesus' death on the cross for his sins. Paul wrote in Galatians 2:21: "I do not nullify the grace of God, for if righteousness *comes* through the Law, then Christ died needlessly."

Paul's transformed life

If the apostle Paul's letters declared his total allegiance to Jesus, his Lord and Master, how is it that Muslims believe otherwise? Louay Fatoohi contends that Paul had no contact with Jesus of Nazareth prior to becoming a Christian. His letters reveal he had "hardly any knowledge of the teachings and history of his religious master yet managing to become the most influential Christian theologian."[25]

Fatoohi was correct that Paul made only a few direct references to the historical Jesus in his writings. But are there relevant factors that Fatoohi has not considered? To the Galatian church, Paul wrote,

> Then three years later I went up to Jerusalem to become acquainted [*historēsai*] with Cephas, and stayed with him fifteen days. But I did not see any other of the apostles except James, the Lord's brother.[26]

Historēsai (from which comes our word "history") is only found here in the entire New Testament. It means "in the common Hellenistic sense of 'visit in order to get to know.'"[27] During the fifteen days Paul spent in Jerusalem, he came with a twofold agenda: (1) he wanted to become aquainted with Peter and James as fellow Christians; most importantly, (2) he wanted firsthand knowledge of Jesus. As his brother, James could provide stories pertaining to his interaction with Jesus within their family setting. On the other hand, Peter could

---

25 Fatoohi, *The Mystery of the Crucifixion*, 63. See also Louay Fatoohi, "Paul's Unhistorical Jesus," *Qur'anic Studies: Writings about the Qur'an, Islam and Religion* (2015); http://www.quranicstudies.com/books/jesus-the-muslim-prophet/pauls-unhistorical-jesus (accessed November 30, 2017).

26 Galatians 1:18–19.

27 Friedrich Büchsel, "*hitorēō (historia)*" in *Theological Dictionary of the New Testament*, ed. Gerhard Kittel and Gerhard Friedrich, trans. Geoffrey W. Bromiley, 10 vols. (Grand Rapids: Eerdmans, 1965), 3:396.

recall how Jesus reacted in a variety of circumstances, having spent three years in ministry with him.

Even though Paul would have found these stories about Jesus to be informative, nevertheless, it was not the historical Jesus that brought about the radical transformation in Paul's life—it was the *risen* Lord Jesus Christ! This was the life-changing message the apostle wanted to communicate through his letters. To Timothy, a young man whom he had mentored, he wrote: "Remember Jesus Christ, risen from the dead, descendant of David, according to my gospel."[28] It should be noted that even when Paul made a historical reference to Jesus—"descendant of David"—he did so within the context of Jesus' resurrection.

Another consideration Fatoohi has overlooked is that the three letters by John and the two by Peter also had little to say about the historical Jesus. Surely this Muslim scholar would not say these two devoted disciples knew little of Jesus' life? Like Paul, they were writing letters to individuals or churches and were dealing with specific moral or spiritual problems. The historicity of Jesus was not the issue.

Ruqaiyyah Maqsood (b. 1942 as Rosalyn Rushbrook) was formerly a British secondary school teacher of Christian religion and is now a prominent advocate of Islam. Even though Maqsood is not able to fathom the spiritual transformation that occurred to Paul on the road to Damascus, she understood the intent of Galatians 2:21 ("I do not nullify the grace of God, for if righteousness comes through the Law, then Christ died needlessly"). She made this pertinent comment: "This solitary sentence [verse] summed up the reason for the continuing vehemence of Christian resistance to Jewish and Muslim theology."[29]

Thomson, speaking on behalf of Muslims, stated: "Paul created Christianity at the expense of those whom Jesus had gathered around him to spread his teachings."[30] In his excellent book, *Paul: Follower of Jesus or Founder of Christianity?*, David Wenham has demonstrated that Thomson's allegation has no credence.[31]

---

28 2 Timothy 2:8.

29 Maqsood, *The Mysteries of Jesus*, 62.

30 Thomson, "The Gospel of Barnabas," *Tell Me about Islam*, 1.2.

31 Wenham, *Paul: Follower of Jesus or Founder of Christianity?*

Certainly, Jesus' resurrection, the cornerstone of Paul's theology, added a new dimension to his message. The apostle Paul was no innovator but he referred to himself as "a bond-servant [*doulos*] of Christ Jesus."[32] Paul's message to his generation was that this *doulos* relationship was available to all who put their faith in Jesus Christ, the risen Lord.

The resurrection was paramount in his teaching: "if Christ has not been raised, then our preaching is vain [*kenon*], your faith is also vain [*kenē*]."[33] This admonition takes on greater meaning when one realizes that *kenē* means "purposeless, hollow and false."[34]

Irenaeus—defender against false teachings

In their fourth chapter, "Early Unitarians in Christianity," Rahim and Thomas devoted a mere four pages to three major early church fathers: Irenaeus, Tertullian and Origen. But it was Irenaeus, as noted by them, who "quoted extensively from the *Gospel of Barnabas*."[35] This statement is blatantly false.

Similar to many of the second-century church fathers, Irenaeus was aware of the Epistle of Barnabas. But none had ever heard of the *Gospel of Barnabas*. Irenaeus authored two books, *Against Heresies* and *The Demonstration of Apostolic Preaching* (*ca.* A.D. 180). Armitage Robinson, who translated Irenaeus' latter work,[36] footnoted eleven citations from the Epistle of Barnabas.

It is obvious that Rahim and Thomson confused the Epistle of Barnabas, a document written in Alexandria, Egypt, between A.D. 70–135 with their so-called *Gospel of Barnabas*. What is even more alarming is that Thomson, having written an article in 2017,[37] still maintained that Irenaeus made reference to the *Gospel of Barnabas*. He did so even though, a few pages later, he notes that the Epistle

---

32 Romans 1:1.

33 1 Corinthians 15:14.

34 *The Analytical Greek Lexicon* (Grand Rapids: Zondervan, 1970), 228.

35 Rahim and Thomson, *Jesus: Prophet of Islam*, 78.

36 See Irenaeus, *The Demonstration of Apostolic Preaching*, trans. and notes Armitage Robinson (New York: Macmillan, 1920); http://www.documentacatholicaomnia. eu/03d/0130-0202,_Iraeneus_Demonstration_Of_The_Apostolic_Preaching,_EN.pdf (accessed April 6, 2017).

37 Thomson, "The Gospel of Barnabas," *Tell Me about Islam*, 1.2.

of Barnabas had been discovered with Codex Sinaiticus, the oldest complete manuscript of the New Testament.[38] Knowing the Epistle of Barnabas existed, why did he not realize, as did other scholars, that the document that Irenaeus had in his possession was the Epistle of Barnabas not the *Gospel of Barnabas*? One can only surmise he is so committed to defending the historicity of *Jesus: Prophet of Islam* for the sake of Islam that he is completely blind to facts that are so obvious to other historians.

Rahim and Thomson were interested in the writings of Irenaeus for another reason. It was he who referred to Basilides (*ca.* A.D. 117–160).[39] They contended that this teacher from Alexandria, Egypt, was one of the first to deny that Jesus was crucified. As a Gnostic, Basilides believed that a crucifixion did occur in A.D. 33 but, since humanity had no need of atonement for their sins, Jesus' death on the cross was unnecessary. Instead he believed:

Simon of Cyrene was compelled to bear the cross in his place, but Simon was transfigured by him, so that Simon was thought to be Jesus. So, through ignorance and error, Simon was crucified, while Jesus took on the appearance of Simon, and, standing by, laughed at them.[40]

When refuting the heretical Gnostic teaching of Basilides, Irenaeus echoed in his *Against Heresies* the same gospel message of Jesus' death, burial and resurrection as did the others before him. This second century theologian wrote:

"With great power," it was added, "the apostles gave their testimony to the resurrection of the Lord Jesus [Acts 4:33], saying to them, "The God of our ancestors raised up Jesus, whom you had killed by hanging him on a tree. God exalted him at his right hand as Leader and Savior."[41]

---

38 Thomson, "The Gospel of Barnabas," *Tell Me about Islam*, 1.2.
39 Rahim and Thomson, *Jesus: Prophet of Islam*, 47.
40 Irenaeus, *Against Heresies*, 1.24.4. See Payton Jr., *Irenaeus on the Christian Faith*, 37.
41 Irenaeus, *Against Heresies*, 3.12.5. See Payton Jr., *Irenaeus on the Christian Faith*, 67.

Irenaeus was helpful in resolving another contentious area. These two Muslim scholars long believed that the rift between Paul and Barnabas was not based upon a difference of opinion concerning John Mark but rather a more serious theological issue: Paul had broken rank with all the disciples, including Peter, because he disregarded the historical Jesus. Commenting some 150 years later, Irenaeus did not see an irreconcilable hostility between Paul and Peter. Rather,

> For he [Paul] said that one and the same God who worked through Peter for the mission of the circumcised worked through himself for the Gentiles. Hence, Peter was the apostle for the same God as Paul; the very God and the Son of God, whom Peter announced to those in circumcision.[42]

Nicene Creed—a defence of Christian orthodoxy

A major misconception of Rahim and Thomson concerning the Nicene Creed was their lack of understanding as to what the bishops were called upon to do. They were not invited to Nicaea by Constantine to enact "official resolutions"[43] or develop new doctrinal teachings. As representatives of the whole church, they were to affirm what had been firmly believed and established since the first century.

A careful examination of the creed itself—something which these Muslim authors failed to do—would reveal the intent of this document. Their main duty was to confirm the long-held doctrine of Jesus Christ's deity. Even though these bishops were trinitarians, their focus was to show that Jesus was indeed "light from light, true God from true God."[44]

The authors of *Jesus: Prophet of Islam* articulated another undocumented assertion that these bishops "who were invited were not on the whole very knowledgeable."[45] They even took this assumption one step further when they stated:

---

42 Irenaeus, *Against Heresies*, 3.13.1. He was referencing Galatians 2:7–10.
43 Rahim and Thomson, *Jesus: Prophet of Islam*, 110.
44 Bray, *Creeds, Councils and Christ*, 116.
45 Rahim and Thomson, *Jesus: Prophet of Islam*, 96.

the majority of the delegates at the Council, did not agree with the doctrine of the Trinity at all, but nevertheless signed the Creed with silent reservation, in order to please the Emperor.[46]

No records have survived concerning the council's deliberations but there is an important fact that should not be overlooked. Many of these bishops had endured the Great Persecution in the early fourth century—one of the greatest trials placed on the early church. These were men of strong character. While they would have respected their emperor, they also possessed deep spiritual convictions. To claim that these bishops remained in "silent reservation" is unsubstantiated by the facts we do know about them.

Rahim's and Thomson's second most blatant fabrication is their allegation that the bishops at the Council of Nicaea were responsible for choosing the four Gospels of the New Testament. They claim that Constantine—"a wicked and calculating man"[47]—arranged for a "miracle" to be performed at Nicaea to convince the gathered bishops that he was acting on behalf of God. Rahim and Thomson state: "According to one source, there were at least 270 versions of the Gospels at this time, while another stated there were as many as 4,000 different Gospels."[48] Which ones were accurate and reliable?

Rahim and Thomson claim that it was agreed that all these various Gospels should be placed under a table in the council hall. The bishops would retire to their rooms and pray that God would miraculously place the true Gospels of Jesus on top of the table. The next morning, "the Gospels most acceptable to Athanasius, the representative of Alexander [bishop of Alexandria]"[49] were the four Gospels of Matthew, Mark, Luke and John which were found neatly lying on the table. Everyone agreed that in order to avoid confusion, all the other gospels which remained under the table should be burned. Having witnessed the intervention of God, the bishops were now ready to be led by Athanasius.

Accompanying the Nicene Creed were twenty canons or decrees that churches were expected to follow. In these twenty directives,

---

46 Rahim and Thomson, *Jesus: Prophet of Islam*, 104.
47 'Abd al-Jabbār, *The Critique of Christianity*, 3.205.
48 Rahim and Thomson, *Jesus: Prophet of Islam*, 105.
49 Rahim and Thomson, *Jesus: Prophet of Islam*, 105.

there is absolutely no mention of what books of the New Testament, or more specifically the four Gospels, were to be accepted as authoritative.

In the minds of Rahim and Thomson, Athanasius in concert with Constantine directed the entire proceedings of the Council of Nicaea. In their brief six-line introductory statement concerning him, they stated,

> Athanasius was a young and fiery supporter of the beliefs and concepts which eventually led to the formation of what became known as the Trinitarian school of theology. Alexander, who was growing old, and had been routed by Arius, decided to send Athanasius to Nicaea as his representative, instead of going himself.[50]

This quotation clearly illustrates how Rahim and Thomson cared little about historical accuracy. This supposed Trinitarian school established by Athanasius never existed. Furthermore, Athanasius was not a bishop; consequently, he would have been unable to take an active role in the proceedings at Nicaea.

Even John Firth (1868–1943), the historian most consulted by Rahim and Thomson, penned these words: "It was Athanasius, who now, as a young deacon of twenty-five, accompanied Alexander to Nicaea."[51] As Firth has correctly stated, Athanasius was not in charge of the Egyptian delegation. There can be no doubt that Alexander had a high regard for his assistant and was grooming him to be his successor. In A.D. 326, one year after the Council of Nicaea, Alexander died and Athanasius donned the bishop's attire. It should also be noted that Firth believed that the Council of Nicaea always wanted Arianism to be recognized as heretical.[52]

During Rahim's and Thomson's discussion of the Nicene Creed in *Jesus: Prophet of Islam*, Arius, as one would expect, is viewed as the champion of orthodoxy. His belief that Jesus was a mere man and not God completely resonates with Islamic theology. Libyan

---

50 Rahim and Thomson, *Jesus: Prophet of Islam*, 97.

51 John Firth, *Constantine the Great: The Reorganization of the Empire and the Triumph of the Church* (Freeport: Books for Libraries Press, 1904), 215.

52 Firth, *Constantine the Great*, 229.

by birth, Arius was a presbyter in Egypt who challenged not only Constantine but also the Christian church of his day. As one who wholeheartedly followed the teachings of Jesus, he adamantly refused to accept Paul's nefarious doctrines. His motto was: "Follow Jesus as he preached."[53]

There was another important fact that Rahim and Thomson deliberately fail to mention. As with all his fourth-century contemporaries, Arius believed that Jesus, a good man, was not only crucified but was resurrected bodily from the dead. Furthermore, a creedal statement endorsed by Arius along with Euzoius (d. A.D. 376), an Arian bishop of Antioch, further validated his belief in the crucifixion and resurrection of Jesus Christ:

> We believe in one God, the Father, the ruler of all; and in the Lord Jesus Christ, his only Son, *the one begotten from him, before all ages,*[54] …the one who descended and took flesh and suffered and rose and ascended into the heavens and is coming again to judge the living and the dead.[55]

To amplify the readers' sympathy for Arius, Rahim and Thomson concocted a mythical tale concerning his death. In A.D. 336, they reported that he died of poisoning and that the church rejoiced. Constantine was convinced that Arius had been murdered. So, "he appointed a commission to investigate the death which had taken place in such a mysterious manner. Athanasius was found to be responsible and was condemned for the murder of Arius."[56]

But much to their chagrin, Rahim and Thomson had to admit that the Niceno-Constantinopolitan Creed in A.D. 381 established the belief that God was triune in nature. Theodosius I, himself a trinitarian, promoted the true understanding of the biblical view of God which the authors of the New Testament had recorded four centuries earlier.

---

53 Rahim and Thomson, *Jesus: Prophet of Islam*, 82.

54 These words were not italicized in the original, but they are highly significant in that they convey the essential Arian doctrine that Jesus was God's first created being.

55 Rowan Williams, *Arius: Heresy and Tradition* (London: Darton, Longman and Todd, 1987), 355–356.

56 Rahim and Thomson, *Jesus: Prophet of Islam*, 108.

Summary

The greatest danger of Rahim's and Thomson's revisionist history is that others have accepted it as fact, particularly Muslims. For instance, Ruqaiyyah Maqsood, whose book *The Mysteries of Jesus: A Study of the Origins and Doctrines of the Christian Church* (2000) was referenced in the last chapter, accepted as historical fact the fabricated account of the selection of the four Gospels as presented by Rahim and Thomson. She also erroneously implicated Athanasius and Constantine:

> The Lord was besought to levitate the inspired volumes on the table, and leave the spurious ones underneath. In the course, those favored by Athanasius were found to have risen upon the table, and Constantine ordered all the rest to be burned.[57]

If a prolific Muslim author of some fourteen religious books can be deceived by such falsehoods, what can be said of the average, uninformed reader? On Amazon.com,[58] there were twelve customers who reviewed the book. Seven gave it either a four- or five-star rating. One wrote: "One of the Greatest Books ever written on Christianity." Another who appeared to be a Muslim made this comment:

> The book explains how the arguments between the early Christians were resolved through the exercise of state power by the Roman Empire at the Council of Nicaea. It also covers how the text of the New Testament was decided and two books excluded from it, The *Gospel of Barnabas* and The Shepherd of Hermas.

One of the two that awarded *Jesus: Prophet of Islam* with one star stated he was a Muslim. He was highly critical of Rahim's reference to the *Gospel of Barnabas*. For him, it was a fourteenth to sixteenth century document. He also disagreed that Irenaeus and Arius were Unitarians.

---

57 Maqsood, *The Mysteries of Jesus*, 199.

58 "*Jesus: Prophet of Islam*: Muhammad 'Ata Ur-Rahim"; https://www.amazon.com/Jesus-Prophet-Muhammad-Ata-Ur-Rahim/dp/1879402734 (accessed February 12, 2019).

The other who also gave a one star noted that Rahim's work was "historically inaccurate." He made this chilling observation: "I could not be more disappointed with the dishonesty of the authors (whether intentional or not I can't say)." Along with the Muslim critic above, he questioned the validity of the *Gospel of Barnabas* and the account of the selection of the Gospels. His last statement was very telling: "If I remember correctly, the only religion which burned the manuscripts of its early texts was Islam under Uthman."

Theodosius I
(A.D. 347–395)

Theodosius I made Christianity the official state religion. In A.D. 391, he enacted edicts against pagan worship. He was the last emperor to reign over both the Eastern and Western halves of the empire.

The most shocking Amazon review was by a medical doctor. This educated man accepted without question Rahim's and Thomson's outrageous narratives of Paul's conversion and the selection of the four Gospels. His concluding comment referring to this last incident was:

> The Unity Bishops hoped that by agreeing to this they could go home and be left alone. It was also agreed that Jesus was the son of God and Divine. Constantine held another conference in 381 that placed the Holy Ghost in with God and Jesus, so now there was a Trinity.[59]

Another obvious historical error was that it was Theodosius I and not Constantine who convened the Council of Constantinople in A.D. 381.

---

59 Nur Randall Hrabko, "Book review: *Jesus: Prophet of Islam*," *Technology of the Heart* (2017); http://www.techofheart.co/2011/10/book-review-jesus-prophet-of-islam-nur.html (accessed December 6, 2017).

CHAPTER 8

Jesus' death on the cross: real or feigned?

The Christian view of Jesus' death—a biblical reality

PRIOR TO JESUS' birth, an angel appeared to Joseph and made this announcement:

> Joseph, son of David, do not be afraid to take Mary as your wife; for the Child who has been conceived in her is of the Holy Spirit. She will bear a Son; and you shall call His name Jesus, for He will save His people from their sins.[1]

The fulfillment of that prophecy occurred when Jesus, of his own volition, allowed malicious men to place him on a cross. It was there that God poured out his wrath in judgement upon his righteous Son to pay the penalty for humanity's rebellion against him.

For Jesus' followers, his death should not have been a surprise. On three different occasions as recorded in each of the Gospels, he clearly outlined his impending death.[2] Nothing could stop his

---

1 Matthew 1:20–21.

2 See Zahniser's excellent description of these nine prophecies in "The Son of Man must be killed: Jesus predicts the end of his mission" in *The Mission and Death of Jesus in Islam and Christianity*, 148–169.

"inescapable mission awaiting him in Jerusalem."[3]

By comparing any harmony of the Gospels, one can see that all of them record that Jesus died on the cross. Furthermore, each of the writers of the Gospels used different expressions to describe Jesus' death:

Mark 15:37—*ekpneō* (literally to breathe out, to expire)
Matthew 27:50—*aphiēmi to pneuma* (to yield [his] spirit)
Luke 23:46—*paratithēmi to pneuma* (to give out [his] spirit)
John 19:30—*paradidomi to pneuma* (to deliver [his] spirit)

Further confirmation is found in Mark's Gospel when Joseph of Arimathea "gathered up courage and went in before Pilate and asked for the body [corpse] of Jesus."[4] Pilate was amazed that Jesus had died so quickly and inquired of the centurion who was in charge and present when Jesus took his last breath (Greek, *exepneueusen*).[5] This experienced Roman soldier had witnessed numerous crucifixions and would know when someone had died. He also testified, "Truly [*alēthōs*] this man was the Son of God."[6] The testimony of these four Gospels, the inspired words of the living God, show that Jesus' death is totally undeniable!

A Jewish delegation approached Pilate to ensure that those crucified would be buried before the Sabbath arrived. "So the soldiers came, and broke the legs of the first man and of the other who was crucified with Him; but coming to Jesus, when they saw that He was already dead, they did not break His legs."[7]

It was at this moment that a soldier thrust his spear into Jesus' dead body. Thus, the *coup de grâce*—the soldier's thrust into Jesus' side[8]—did not kill Jesus as he was already dead.

---

3   L.D. Hurst and J.B. Green, "Predictions of Jesus' Passion and Resurrection," in Green, McKnight and Marshall, eds., *Dictionary of Jesus and the Gospels*, 630.

4   Mark 15:43.

5   Mark 15:39.

6   Mark 15:39. See the prologue in Ignatius of Antioch, *To the Smyrneans*, where he uses *alēthōs* three times in his description of Jesus' lineage, his virgin birth and finally his crucifixion and resurrection.

7   John 19:32–33.

8   John 19:34.

Tetelestai (Greek, perfect passive of *teleō*), meaning it is finished, was the word "written on business documents or receipts in New Testament times to show that a bill had been paid in full."[9] In John's Gospel,[10] this single word uttered from the cross by Jesus signified that he had fulfilled his mission as announced by the angel at his birth. Through his death, burial and resurrection, he paid in full humanity's sin debt. Now, there was a legitimate way in which individuals through faith and repentance could be reconciled to a holy and righteous God.

Joel Green writes in his book, *The Death of Jesus*, "For these reasons the death of Jesus on the cross can be looked upon as a historical occurrence with virtual certainty."[11]

The Islamic view of Jesus' death—three options

All Muslims believe that a crucifixion occurred but the question to be answered is: How was Jesus spared from this humiliating death? In the first two of three options, each has a different English translation of the Arabic, *shubbiha lahum*, found in Sura 4:157.

1. Substitutionary option

And for their [Jews'] saying, "Surely we killed the Messiah, Jesus, son of Mary, the messenger of God"—yet they did not kill him, nor did they crucify him, but [*another*] *was made to resemble him to them*. And indeed, those who differ over it are in doubt about it.[12]

The Arabic rendering, *shubbiha lahum*— "[another] was made to resemble him to them"—is the basis of the substitutionary option.

After distributing the tract, "Jesus and the Qur'an," to Muslims near the mosque in London, Ontario, I met a postgraduate student

---

9 "What does the Greek word "*tetelestai*" mean?" Bible.org. (2017); https://bible.org/question/what-does-greek-word-tetelestai-mean (accessed March 2, 2017).

10 John 19:30

11 Joel B. Green, *The Death of Jesus: Tradition and Interpretation in the Passion Narrative* (Tübingen: J.C.B. Mohr, 1988), 1.

12 *The Qur'an: English Meaning and Notes* (Riyadh: Saheen International, 2012), Sura 4:157. Italics added.

in health sciences at the University of Western Ontario. He agreed to complete my questionnaire.[13] In answering the first question, he believed that someone died in Jesus' place on the cross. He was not aware of the *Gospel of Barnabas* and its declaration that Judas was the one who took Jesus' place.

This university student would be in agreement with Fatoohi who wrote,

> While [Sura 4:157] clearly means that someone else was mistaken for Jesus and killed, there is nothing in this verse or anywhere in the Qur'an that supports or justifies any attempt to identify that person.[14]

Sura 53:38 says, "That no one bearing a burden bears the burden for another."[15] This Qur'anic verse captures the belief of this postgraduate student. No one else could endure punishment for the sins of another. Everyone is totally responsible for his or her own sins. Thus, God would not permit Jesus to experience the shame and ignominy of crucifixion, especially by the evil designs of his enemies.

Having established his position concerning Jesus' death, I turned his attention to the last question in the questionnaire about death. From the seven options listed,[16] he chose the second option: heaven or hell. He, like the majority of Muslims, have no knowledge of what would happen after they die.

This university student stated that there were a number of considerations that had to be addressed before one's eternal destiny can be finalized. He believed that when he died he would go to *Barzakh* —something akin to purgatory in Roman Catholic theology. There, while he is awaiting the Day of Judgement, family and friends could pray for him and do good works on his behalf.

At the end of time, Allah must evaluate his life—whether it was marked by good or bad deeds—and also the merit built up by others

---

13 Interview #644 (October 20, 2017).

14 Fatoohi, *The Mystery of the Crucifixion*, 107.

15 See A.J. Droge's comment on the verse in footnote 34: "i.e. judgment falls on individuals, whom neither family nor friends can help (an implicit rejection of the Christian doctrine of vicarious [substitutionary] atonement."

16 Consult the Appendix to find all the options.

on his behalf. Then and only then could he truly know whether his final destination will be heaven or hell.

Counter arguments

It was my privilege to share with this affable student that I too believed in God's substitutionary plan. As one destined to eternal damnation because of my blatant disregard for God's law, I too needed a substitute. Mine was Jesus Christ, the God-man. The punishment that I justly deserved was taken by Jesus. The Bible makes this marvelous claim,

> He [God] made Him [Jesus] who knew no sin *to be* sin on our behalf, so that we might become the righteousness of God in Him.[17]

In his latest book, *The Qur'an and the Historical Jesus*, South African lawyer John Gilchrist outlined how Gnosticism was the original source for the substitutionary theory:

> The Gnostic teaching that the Christ was a figure who had come from heaven and who had no physical form but only took on the human Jesus is an adaptation of the early heresy known as docetism.… From this error the substitution theory developed until it found its ultimate home in the Quranic teaching about a likeness, a twin-image, being substituted for the real Jesus as he was raised up to heaven.[18]

Gilchrist also mentioned that an eighth-century Muslim historian, Muhammad Ibn Ishaq (A.D. 704–*ca.* 770), recorded that Sergius—deemed to be the thirteenth disciple—volunteered to take Jesus' place.[19] In his study, he also mentions the impact of Arianism on the Qur'an. His conclusion was that the Islamic Jesus was "in every case reshaped, reinvented and shorn of his glory."[20]

---

17 2 Corinthians 5:21. Italics in the original.

18 John Gilchrist, *The Qur'an and the Historical Jesus* (Benoni: Christian Resources Ministries, 2015), 81.

19 Gilchrist, *The Qur'an and the Historical Jesus*, 75.

20 Gilchrist, *The Qur'an and the Historical Jesus*, 142.

American Muslim scholar, Mahmoud Ayoub has been critical of the substitutionary explanation because an innocent person like Simon of Cyrene or Judas was subjected to the cruel punishment of crucifixion. Such an act could not be ordained by God. Ayoub felt that this approach of explaining Jesus' death gained popularity because "one of the disciples voluntarily accepted death as a ransom for his master."[21]

2. Resuscitation or "swoon theory"

> And for their [Jews'] saying, "Surely we killed the Messiah, Jesus, son of Mary, the messenger of God"—yet they did not kill him, nor did they crucify him, but *it (only) seemed like (that) to them*. Surely those who differ about him are indeed in doubt about him.[22]

The Arabic rendering, *shubbiha lahum*, in italics—"*it (only) seemed like (that) to them*"—is the basis of the resuscitation or "swoon theory."

The "swoon theory" from a Western perspective

During the eighteenth and nineteenth centuries, the reliability of the Bible came under attack. Jesus' miracles and his resurrection were subject to naturalistic explanations. An early proponent of this naturalistic approach was Karl Friedrich Bahrdt (1741–1792).

An unorthodox German theologian, Bahrdt proposed that Luke, a physician, administered drugs which put Jesus into a comma and allowed him to feign death. Later, Jesus was resuscitated by Joseph of Arimathea. Bahrdt claimed that on the third day, "his appearance scared away the guards at the tomb and he went to live in isolation with the Essenes."[23] Two German rationalists also adopted the "swoon theory": Karl Heinrich Venturini (1768–1849) and Heinrich Paulus (1761–1851).[24]

---

21 Ayoub, *A Muslim View of Christianity*, 161.

22 Sura 4:157. This is A.J. Droge's interpretation.

23 Frederick T. Zugibe, *The Crucifixion of Jesus: A Forensic Inquiry* (New York: M. Evans, 2005), 146.

24 For more detail, see Zia H. Shah, "The swoon hypothesis," *The Muslim Times: Fostering Universal Brotherhood in Our Global Village* (2016); https://themuslimtimes. info/2016/03/26/the-swoon-hypothesis-2/comment-page-1/ (accessed December 12, 2017).

Those aligning themselves with the "swoon theory" did not abate during the twentieth and twenty-first centuries. Two notable books are: *The Anastasis: The Resurrection of Jesus as an Historical Event* (Drinkwater, 1982) by J. Duncan M. Derrett and *The Passover Plot: A New Interpretation of the Life and Death of Jesus* (Bantam, 1971) by Hugh J. Schonfield. How reliable are these testimonies? Frederick Zugibe (1928–2013), the first chief medical examiner in Rockland County, New York, made this assessment in his book *The Crucifixion of Jesus: A Forensic Inquiry*. Dr. Zugibe contended that the entire process of Jesus' death, including the scourging, was much too intense for Jesus to have survived. Futhermore, he noted, "No drugs were capable of placing him into a deep sleep to feign death given his condition."[25]

The "swoon theory" from an Islamic perspective

Mirza Ghulam Ahmad (1835–1908), founder of the unorthodox Ahmadiyya Movement in Islam, adopted "the swoon theory" in his book, *Jesus in India* (1899). Based on his understanding of Matthew 12:40, Ahmad believed God could deliver Jesus in the same way he had delivered Jonah from the belly of the whale.

According to this Indian author, it was Joseph of Arimathea and Pilate who engineered Jesus' deliverance from the cross. He wrote:

> Jesus was declared dead and his body was placed in his custody. Since Joseph was a respected personality, the Jews could not quarrel with him. Thus, he took charge of Jesus, who had been declared dead whereas he was actually in a coma. Following Pilate's instructions, he took Jesus to a room with an opening which was used as a grave according to the prevailing custom of the time, and was beyond the access of the Jews.[26]

Once revived, Jesus met with his disciples and Pilate in Galilee. He presented to them his wounds and that he was indeed alive. After this brief encounter, he fled to Kashmir where he later died.

---

25 Zugibe, *The Crucifixion of Jesus*, 161.

26 Hadrat Mirza Ghulam Ahmad, *Jesus in India: Jesus' Deliverance from the Cross & Journey to India* (Punjab: Islam International Publications (2016), 32; https://www.alislam. org/library/books/Jesus-in-India.pdf (accessed December 12, 2017).

Nabeel Qureshi (1984–2017) was born into an extremely devoted Ahmadi Muslim family. It was they who used the term "theistic swoon theory." The Arabic phrase, *shubbiha lahum*—"made to appear so to them"—indicated that God intervened and miraculously resuscitated Jesus.

To bolster this argument, Qureshi referred to the prayers of Jesus in the Garden of Gethsemane. In his anxiety concerning his impending crucifixion, Jesus "implored God to save him from the cross."[27] Moved with compassion, God set in motion a rescue plan.

In 2005, Nebeel dedicated his life to Jesus Christ. He graduated from Eastern Virginia Medical School and eventually left the medical profession to join Ravi Zacharias International Ministries (RZIM). As a persuasive apologist, he defended the Christian message around the world. In 2016, he was diagnosed with stomach cancer.

On September 16, 2017, Nabeel's battle with cancer ended—he is now in the presence of his Lord! In his final video, posted just eight days before his death, he said, "I think God understands where I am right now, and he comes alongside us in that, and he loves us and gives us the strength."[28]

During a debate with New Testament scholar Michael Licona, Shabir Ally, a Canadian and noted defender of Islam, mentioned that the Qur'an was correct in stating that Jews were not responsible for Jesus' death. In reality, it was Romans who orchestrated it. Ally clearly articulated his commitment to a "theistic swoon theory."

Nabeel Qureshi (1984–2017)

Qureshi wrote two inspiring books that highlighted his spiritual journey. *Seeking Allah, Finding Jesus* focused on his conversion to Christianity. His second, *No God but One: Allah or Jesus?* centred on his realization that a true understanding of the nature of Jesus, the God-man, could only be found in Christianity.

---

27 Nabeel Qureshi, *No God but One: Allah or Jesus? A Former Muslim Investigates the Evidence for Islam and Christianity* (Grand Rapids: Zondervan, 2006), 172.

28 Kate Shellnut, "Died: Nabeel Qureshi, Author of 'Seeking Allah, Finding Jesus'" *Christianity Today* (September 16, 2017); http://www.christianitytoday.com/news/2017/september/died-nabeel-qureshi-author-seeking-allah-finding-jesus-rzim.html (accessed September 21, 2017).

First, he left no doubt that God was in control:

> I will take the view that he [Jesus] was actually rescued and that he did not actually die but *he was taken down alive from the cross*. He was placed in a tomb. From that tomb, he was translated to heaven.[29]

He also stated that Jesus was alive when he was taken down from the cross:

> If he was taken either in a state of sleep or death, this would not contradict the Qur'an. While the Qur'an in 4:158 affirms that God raised Jesus, the timing and manner of that raising is not specified.[30]

Counter argument

In "Blood, water and the end of the swoon theory," a chapter in *The Crucifixion of Jesus*, Zugibe convincingly presented evidence that Jesus did indeed die on a cross. Consequently, he concluded that "the swoon theory" was without a doubt a hoax.

Having been a medical examiner for thirty-four years, Zugibe examined every conceivable cause of death. He confessed, however, that

> none compared to the intricacies that confronted me during my probe into the death of Jesus. In a sense, the process was like conducting an autopsy across the centuries.[31]

After nearly four decades of research, Zugibe came to the conclusion that Jesus died of a heart rupture. It was precipitated by three traumatic experiences: the sweating of blood (*hematidrosis*) in the

---

29 "Jesus was crucified and then rescued: Dr. Shabir Ally," (September 10, 2016); https://www.youtube.com/watch?v=9L8FVuVbSSs (accessed February 24, 2017). Italics added.

30 Shabir Ally, "Did Jesus Physically Rise from the Dead? An Evaluation of the Craig/Ally Debate," (April 12, 2009); https://shabirally.wordpress.com/2009/04/12/did-jesus-physically-rise-from-the-dead/ (accessed February 23, 2017).

31 Zugibe, *The Crucifixion of Jesus*, 1–2.

Garden of Gethsemane, the Roman scourging and the actual crucifixion. The conclusive evidence was in John 19:34: "But one of the soldiers pierced His side with a spear, and immediately blood and water came out."

Dr. Zugibe reasoned that Jesus died prior to the spear thrust. First, as a result of cardiac arrest, the heart's last contraction filled the right atrium with blood. Second, the hours of beatings would have caused an accumulation of fluid around the lungs. Thus,

> the quick, jerking motion used to pull out the spear then carried out blood that had adhered to the blade and some of the effusion (water) from the pleural (lung) cavity, resulting in the phenomenon of "blood and water."[32]

3. Death of the Islamic Jesus—theological not historical

Mahmoud Ayoub was born in South Lebanon in 1935. After receiving his undergraduate degree in his home country, he went to the United States where he attended the University of Pennsylvania where he obtained his masters, and then Harvard for his doctorate.

His teaching career spanned nearly four decades and was spent in both the United States and Canada. As a result of his close association with the Western academic world, he developed educational programs to promote better understanding and cooperation between Christianity and Islam.

To enhance this ecumenical spirit, Ayoub formulated his own view of Jesus' death. First, he posed this pertinent question,

> Why, then, it must be asked, does the Qur'an deny the crucifixion of Christ in the face of apparently overwhelming evidence? Muslim commentators have not been able convincingly to disprove the crucifixion.[33]

Efforts by Muslim scholars to understand Suras 4:157–158 by using the substitutionary theory have been futile. Instead, Ayoub argued that one should not regard these passages as being *historical*

---

32 Zugibe, *The Crucifixion of Jesus*, 140.
33 Ayoub, *A Muslim View of Christianity*, 176.

but rather view them solely on *theological* grounds. The essence of these qur'anic verses is that the Jews tried to kill Jesus who represented the Word of God who was sent to earth. It was Jewish arrogance to declare that they could do so. But they failed. How could anyone destroy the Word of God? Ayoub stated,

> Thus, the denial of the killing of Jesus is a denial of the power of human beings to vanquish and destroy the divine Word, which is forever victorious.[34]

Ayoub was thoroughly convinced that only by negating the *historical* relevance of these texts and focusing on the *theological* interpretation could one achieve inter-religious dialogue. In both Christianity and Islam, Jesus is seen as the Word of God. He concluded,

> Let God be God, not only in His vast creation but in our little lives as well. Then and only then could man be truly man, and the light of God would shine with perfect splendor in our mouths and hearts.[35]

Counter argument

Christian theologians recognize that God's message from Genesis to Revelation can be referred to as "salvation history." When Adam and Eve, of their own free will, determined to disobey God's direct command, their descendants (all humanity) were placed under the power of sin. This condition of rebellion means we are all under the judgement of God.

Such condemnation has dire consequences—eternal separation from God, namely hell. Realizing that humanity had no ability to save themselves, God provided a means for their salvation by sending his Son, Jesus Christ. As the God-man, he entered into history when he was born in Bethlehem around 5 B.C. Just over three decades later, Jesus died on a Roman cross to provide salvation to men and women who so desperately needed it.

---

34 Ayoub, *A Muslim View of Christianity*, 176.
35 Ayoub, *A Muslim View of Christianity*, 177.

Unlike Ayoub's solution of discarding history and only emphasizing theology, the Bible maintains both. In Galatians 4:4–5, the apostle Paul captured the essence of salvation history in two words, *sent* and *redeem*:

> But when the fullness of the time came, God *sent* forth His Son, born of a woman, born under the Law, so that He might *redeem* those who were under the Law, that we might receive the adoption as sons.

Conclusion

Evaluating new information of past events

HISTORY IS THE study of the past but, as time progresses, new information concerning historical events often comes to light. It is the task of historians to evaluate this new data and determine its veracity. When there is a consensus within the historical community that the new source of information is valid, it will then become part of accepted historical tradition.

The Ultra Secret, authored by Frederick Winterbotham (1897–1990), was the first description of the British Secret Service's decoding of Germany's Enigma messaging machine during the Second World War. This amazing feat was given a special security classification: "Ultra." Written in 1974, Winterbotham's personal account broke nearly three decades of silence.[1]

Stationed at Bletchley Park, a stately mansion located some 80 kilometres (50 miles) northwest of London, England, RAF Group Captain Winterbotham was given the daily responsibility of delivering important decrypted messages to the prime minister, Winston Churchill (1874–1965):

---

[1]   Frederick W. Winterbotham, *The Ultra Secret* (New York: Harper & Row, 1974), 26.

Whether listening in on the lethal U-boat wolf-packs; analyzing the supply lines of Rommel's panzer divisions in the North African desert…the codebreakers seized an invaluable advantage; a means of penetrating into the heart of the German strategy and tactical thinking.[2]

To accomplish this herculean task, they developed "the world's first programmable computers."[3] Now that the information these codebreakers were able to provide to the Allied commanders has been analyzed, historians are able to more accurately assess the plans and strategies used to defeat Hitler and his Nazi regime.

Winterbotham believed that when students are taught the history of World War II, the enormous contribution of Bletchley Park to the war effort should be highlighted. He noted,

…no history of World War II would be complete which did not take into account our knowledge of our enemy's intentions, disclosed by our "most secret source."[4]

Unfortunately, there is a negative side to the evaluation of past events. There are those who deliberately distort or even deny accepted historical accounts for ideological or religious reasons. Individuals who promote this revisionist history persistently misrepresent—and even manipulate—the historical evidence to advance their own purposes.

The denial of the Holocaust of World War II is a classic example of historical revisionism. The motivation for this disturbing ideology has been a distrust of and hatred for Israel. Mehnaz Afridi, director of Holocaust, Genocide and Interfaith Education at Manhattan College, New York, has written *Shoah through Muslim Eyes* in order to dismantle such a distortion of history.

In spite of malicious resistance from both Jewish and Muslim quarters, Afridi persistently confronts the fallacies of Holocaust

---

2   Sinclair McKay, *The Lost World of Bletchley Park: An Illustrated History of the Code-Breaking Centre* (London: Aurum Press, 2013), 8–9.

3   "The Keys to the Reich," (May 5, 2013); https://www.youtube.com/watch?v= iQOnkYVnptE&t=49s (accessed April 29, 2017).

4   Winterbotham, *The Ultra Secret*, 1.

revisionism. In the introduction to her book, she made this compelling response:

> As a guardian of *Shoah* [Holocaust] memory and my commitment to survivors, criticism stings, yet it also triggers self-examination. I delved deeply into my soul and asked myself what business I actually had teaching about the *Shoah*. But all I could think of was how important lessons of the *Shoah* had been to me and how many survivors had trusted me by sharing their own memories of pain and humiliation. Their act of sharing imposed a responsibility on me.[5]

True to her word, Afridi recalled the experiences of three Jewish Holocaust survivors in her book.[6] Each one brought forth the personal reality of the heart wrenching horrors of these death camps.

In 2007, while attending a conference in Munich, Afridi and her husband and daughter visited the Nazi concentration camp at Dachau. Why did this Muslim scholar feel morally obligated to witness *firsthand* this repugnant place of death? She wrote poignantly about the visit,

Shoah through Muslim Eyes

Shoah, a Hebrew word meaning "calamity" or "destruction," has now become identified with the Holocaust perpetrated by the Nazis during World War II. On the gate to the concentration camp at Dachau are the words *Arbeit Macht Frei*, which means "Work sets you free." After interviewing Holocaust survivors, Mehnaz Afridi has shown the absolute mockery of these words.

> Perhaps I wanted to be a witness, a Muslim witness, who could testify against the outrage of Holocaust denial in the Islamic

---

5   Afridi, *Shoah through Muslim Eyes*, x.

6   Afridi, "The Document" in *Shoah through Muslim Eyes*, 93–142. The first to be interviewed was Robert Clary (1926–), born as Robert Max Widerman in Paris, France. He was released from Buchenwald concentration camp on April 1, 1945. He is most remembered as Corporal LeBeau in the popular 1960s sitcom *Hogan's Heroes*.

world and point out the deep danger in ignoring history and the memory of narrative....I went as an act of simple respect for the dead.[7]

Similarly, the spirit of Holocaust deniers surfaced in Muhammad 'Ata ur-Rahim's and Ahmad Thomson's *Jesus: Prophet of Islam*. As revisionist historians, these two Muslim authors are guilty of the Islamicization of Christian history from the first century to the twentieth century. Their primary motivation was to harmonize a seventh-century Islamic teaching that Jesus did *not* die on the cross[8] within a well-established framework of Christian history. Broad and extensive scholarship overwhelmingly stands against this denial of the death of Jesus on a cross.

The Mystery of the Crucifixion

Author Louay Fatoohi believes that someone died on the cross in Jesus' place. He maintains that since Jesus was not well known in Jerusalem his substitute could easily have been mistaken for Jesus. Prior to the actual crucifixion, Fatoohi says God miraculously rescued Jesus.

Not bound by the objectivity of the readily available primary sources, Rahim and Thomson became masters at contriving a historical narrative that is both distorted and perverted. Their disregard for biblical truth was most evident in the ribald description of the apostle Paul's conversion. Not only was it outlandish but it bordered blasphemy!

Both Islam and Christianity agree that Pontius Pilate was the Roman governor at the time of Jesus' crucifixion. The crucial difference between the two is this question: Did Jesus die on the cross by Pilate's order? All the gospel accounts bear witness that he did.

By brushing aside the canonical Gospels, Rahim and Thomson put forward the historicity of the *Gospel of Barnabas* as the foundational document to their Islamicization of Christian history. They

---

7   Afridi, *Shoah through Muslim Eyes*, 95.
8   Sura 1:157–158.

did so in spite of overwhelming evidence to the contrary by both non-Muslim and Muslim historians who contend it was written around the fourteenth century. As noted earlier, fellow Islamic historian 'Abd al-Jabbār made no mention of this "so called" gospel.

The cover of Fatoohi's *The Mystery of the Crucifixion: The Attempt to Kill Jesus in the Qur'an, New Testament, and Historical Sources* epitomizes not only the theme of his book but also the one written by Rahim and Thomson. The image shows Jesus ascending to heaven and another man hanging on the cross—an innocent man, no less! The Latin word *ignotus* is inscribed above his head. "This word means 'unknown,' stressing that it was not Jesus who was crucified, but an unknown man."[9] The Islamicization of Christian history is clearly depicted in this book cover.

In an interview with Afridi, the *New York Times* reporter Samuel Freeman wrote,

> And when there's so much daily tension between Muslims and Jews, it's momentous for us to do this work, whether it's me [*sic*] with *Shoah,* or it's a Jewish scholar speaking out about Muslims in Bosnia or about Palestinian suffering. We are commanded by God to speak the truth.[10]

The same motivation—a search for truth—that prompted Afridi to protect the integrity of Holocaust history can be said of the research for my book. Our cherished understanding of the history of Christianity is under attack by Muslim revisionists. Not committed to historical integrity, they have a single focus—to align Christian history with *their* theological interpretation of the Qur'anic text Sura 4:157.

---

9   Fatoohi, *The Mystery of the Crucifixion,* back of title page.

10   Samuel G. Freeman, "Muslim Scholar, Looking to 'Speak the Truth,' Teaches the Holocaust and Islam," *The New York Times* (February 20, 2015); https://www.nytimes.com/2015/02/21/us/muslim-scholar-looking-to-speak-the-truth-teaches-about-holocaust-and-islam.html (accessed July 27, 2017).

Appendix

Questionnaire: *Jesus' death on the cross—Christian or Muslim views*

Religious preference

ON MAY 30, 2015, a Muslim elementary school teacher from Libya was the first person to complete the questionnaire concerning Christianity and Islam. As shown in Table 1, individuals who were interviewed held a diversity of religious beliefs.

This questionnaire, along with four previous ones,[1] did not adhere to the rigorous scientific standards of a survey. Its main purpose was to discover certain trends. For all five questionnaires that we have done, the interviewees were randomly approached either outside the gates of the University of Western Ontario (UWO) or in Victoria Park in the heart of London, Ontario. One major difference with this particular questionnaire is that the interviewers also went door-to-door in southeast London for the first time. Fifty-one percent of the respondents were from that area of the city.

One constant that has remained over the years is the number of people who have declared themselves as having *no* religious affiliation.

---

[1] Each of these questionnaires was used in my books: *Eternity before Their Eyes* (1,200 people—January 2005–March 2007); *Charles Darwin's Religious Views* (350 people—March 2007–April 2008); *Key to Understanding Origins* (513 people—Nov. 2009–December 2009); *Becoming God: Transhumanism and the Quest for Cybernetic Immortality* (800 people—August 2011–May 2014).

Table 1. Religious preference of respondents.

Roman Catholic	150	Aboriginal Canadians	5
Protestants	145	Jewish	4
None/not stated	129	Eritrean Orthodox	3
Atheist	52	Greek Orthodox	3
Agnostics	50	Janist	1
Muslim	48	Romanian Orthodox	1
Evangelicals	46	Russian Orthodox	1
Theist	19	Baha'i	1
Spiritual	13	Gnostic	1
Higher Power	10	Radhasoami	1
Hindu	9	Sikh	1
Buddhist	6	Astrological	1
		Total	700

The average of the five questionnaires is 19.6%. In 2011, Statistics Canada conducted a survey which found that 23.9% of Canadians viewed themselves as non-religious. Interestingly, in 2001, it was 16.5% and, in 1991, 12%.[2]

Jesus made this statement in his Sermon on the Mount:

> Enter through the narrow gate; for the gate is wide and the way is broad that leads to destruction, and there are many who enter through it. For the gate is small and the way is narrow that leads to life, and there are few who find it.[3]

Jesus' words that only a small group of people will enter the gates of heaven has been borne out by the five questionnaires. In each of the questionnaires, the term *evangelical* was used to designate this select

---

2   David Herbert, *Becoming God: Transhumanism and the Quest for Cybernetic Immortality* (Kitchener: Joshua Press, 2014),148.

3   Matthew 7:13–14.

group. The apostle Paul wrote that God called out certain individuals and transformed them into "a new creation."[4] Jesus spoke of the same process when he said, "You must be born again."[5] The term *evangelical* aptly describes those individuals who have the assurance of eternal life as a result of Jesus' death for their sins.

Throughout the five questionnaires, including the present one, the number of evangelicals has ranged from 5.1% to 7.1%. This present study is 6.6%. These figures are truly indicative of a spiritual reality which Jesus had predicted.

Question 1

Are you aware that Muslims believe that Jesus was not executed on the cross but rather God rescued Jesus from this horrific death?

Yes	143	20%
No	557	80%

An overwhelming number of Londoners have very little knowledge about Islam. The Islamic teaching that Jesus was not crucified was a total surprise to the majority of people. A business administrator learned about Jesus' rescue from the cross through her interaction with a Muslim colleague.[6]

A highly qualified Muslim couple, one a medical doctor and the other an engineer,[7] being well-versed in Islamic theology, firmly believed that Jesus was not crucified. In a nearby home, a devout Muslim neighbor held the same conviction.[8] In a separate conversation with her daughter, a fourth-year student at UWO, it was discovered that she was not aware that Muslims believed that Jesus was not executed on the cross.[9]

---

4 Galatians 6:15.
5 John 3:7.
6 Interview #103 (August 29, 2015).
7 Interviews #14 and #15 (June 6, 2015).
8 Interview #10 (June 6, 2015).
9 Interview #11 (June 6, 2015).

Question 2

The four gospels of the New Testament and ancient non-Christian historians record that Jesus Christ was put to death by Pontius Pilate, the governor of Judea, during the reign of the Roman Emperor Tiberius.

For you, personally, do the above testimonies confirm that Jesus' death on the cross is a historical fact?

Yes	434	62%
No	109	16%
No opinion	157	22%

That only 62% believed that Jesus' death was historically true clearly shows that the knowledge of the Bible has declined in Western civilization. An agnostic doctoral political science student denied the existence of Jesus; he had total distrust for any ancient writings, most definitely the Bible.[10] *The Da Vinci Code* (2003) by novelist Dan Brown (1964–) persuaded a skeptical retired office manager that the New Testament was an unreliable historical source.[11]

An imam stated that he believed that Jesus did not die on the cross; possibly, it was Judas who took his place. This Muslim cleric acknowledged that the Qur'an was not written until the seventh century. Even if the historical accounts between the first and seventh centuries stated that Jesus was crucified, the Qur'an, the infallible Word of God, has the authority to declare that all recorded history is wrong.[12]

Individuals who chose the "no opinion" option had little confidence in the four Gospels. They often mentioned that they were unfamiliar with Pontius Pilate and even Emperor Tiberius.

Question 3a

This questionnaire is focused on important religious issues. How would you define the word, religion?

The question brought forth some interesting responses. A Hindu student, having graduated with a master of engineering degree in

---

10 Interview #68 (July 24, 2015).

11 Interview #71 (August 1, 2015).

12 The discussion occurred August 12, 2016.

India and now completing his second master's degree at UWO, gave one such answer. He believed that all religions were man-made. Their main objective was to enable people to cope with suffering and eventually to bring happiness.[13]

A common atheistic approach to religion was that it was highly institutionalized for the purpose of controlling its parishioners. Many who were former Roman Catholics articulated this viewpoint.[14] The most curt response was that religion was purely a business. The young man, raised Roman Catholic, pointed out that his former church and televangelists were the most culpable.[15]

A second-year history student defined religion as a system of belief based on the three Eternal Questions: Where did we come from?, Why are we here? and Where are we going? I asked him where he had learned this explanation; he told me that he was taught this in a grade 12 philosophy course.[16] My book *Eternity before Their Eyes* is based upon the same premises.

Question 3b

Do you consider yourself to be religious?

Yes	370	53.0%
No	235	33.5%
Not certain	95	13.5%

A second-year atheistic engineering student was convinced that religion would become obsolete and would cease to be in the future. He was astounded to find out that 53% still considered themselves to be religious.[17]

There was a great deal of confusion over this question. A young woman, declaring herself to be evangelical,[18] chose the option that

---

13 Interview #203 (November 26, 2015).

14 Interview #81 (August 14, 2015); Interview #236 (January 15, 2015) and Interview #334 (May 25, 2016).

15 Interview #591 (July 14, 2017).

16 Interview #202 (November 26, 2015).

17 The interview (#117) was conducted on September 9, 2015.

18 The interview (#682) was conducted on December 16, 2017.

she was "not certain" whether she was indeed religious or not. She had definitely committed her life to serve and worship Jesus Christ.

In her view, religious individuals were those who believed that they will inherit eternal life by being good people and serving others. They had no concern about biblical truth.

Furthermore, it has become even more confusing since people want to be considered spiritual rather than religious. In unraveling the term, religion, I have found it helpful for some when I mentioned that I believed that all societies are religious. Each has been in search of answers dealing with the three Eternal Questions of life. This approach concentrates on how individuals think and not on how or what they perform.

Question 4

Death is a reality to be faced by all. What, do you think, would happen to you if you died today?

Heaven	199
Heaven or hell	70
Purgatory to heaven	48
Reincarnation	57
Cessation of existence	99
I do not know	180
Other	47
Total	700

When confronted with the choices after death, a medical practitioner wanted either heaven or reincarnation.[19] His preference was the latter; this aspect of eastern religion always intrigued him as he liked the concept of progressing from one spiritual level to another throughout the course of time. Since he could choose only one option, he decided on heaven. Consistent with his mainline liberal Protestant denomination, he believed that all religions were the

---

19 Interview #549 (April 26, 2017).

product of human ingenuity. The biblical view of sin was unreason-
able to him. It was also inconceivable to accept the biblical truth that
one sin would send a person to hell forever.[20]

A Muslim, having graduated in engineering from an African
country, selected heaven or hell.[21] This choice was very typical of
individuals committed to the Islamic faith. At death, he believed that
he would go to a place called *Barzakh,* something akin to the Roman
Catholic purgatory. At the time of judgement, God would assess his
good deeds against his evil ones. Based on God's determination, he
would either be sent to heaven or hell. In talking to Muslims, one
can see why they have absolutely no assurance where they will
spend eternity. In the final analysis, it is dependent on their ability
to please God.

One July 2017 evening while conducting interviews at Victoria
Park, I met three men who identified their religious preference as
being Roman Catholic. In answering the question related to death,
they responded differently. The first believed that no one could ever
know[22] while the second chose the cessation of existence.[23] The third
felt that he was going to heaven.[24] He was totally unaware of the
biblical teaching that one could be assured of eternal life through
Jesus Christ. I was somewhat surprised that the third, a committed
Catholic, did not believe that he must spend time in purgatory before
entering heaven.

Depending on the situation, I took every opportunity to inform
Roman Catholics that the Bible does not teach the doctrine of purgatory. Roman Catholic theologian Brett Salkeld must be commended
for stating:

> Evangelicals are correct to reject any arguments by Catholic
> apologists that seem to suggest that some passages in the New
> Testament indicate a fully formed doctrine in the early Christian
> communities that could rightly be called purgatory.[25]

---

20 Romans 3:23.

21 Interview #522 (March 14, 2017).

22 Interview #591 (July 14, 2017).

23 Interview #592 (July 14, 2017).

24 Interview #593 (July 14, 2017).

25 Brett Salkeld, *Can Catholics and Evangelicals Agree about Purgatory and the Last Judgment?* (Mahwah: Paulist Press, 2011), 35.

Salkeld also indicated that it was not until the time of Gregory the Great (*ca.* A.D. 540–604) that the teaching of purgatory took root and flourished during the Middle Ages.[26] But at the time of the Council of Trent (1545–1563)—a reaction to the Protestant Reformation—purgatory became enshrined within Roman Catholic dogma as the accepted theological position.[27]

For Salkeld, purgatory is best understood as the final step in the process of sanctification which began at birth. Thus, it should be seen as "the doorway to heaven…the beginning of heaven, or one's first experience of heaven."[28]

The adoption of purgatory by the Roman Catholic Church has established a non-biblical understanding of Jesus' vicarious death on the cross. The author of the book of Hebrews stated,

By this will we have been sanctified (*hēgiasmenoi*) through the offering of the body of Jesus Christ once for all (*ephapax*).[29]

At Calvary, Jesus' death completed—once for all, in full measure—sanctification for all believers. At the moment one is born into the family of God through faith in Jesus Christ, he takes up residence in the life of every believer. The Bible now refers to this person as a saint (*hagios*) or sanctified one.[30] Jesus' perfection has become his or hers. In light of this new standing, Paul wrote:

By His [God's] doing you are in Christ Jesus, who became to us wisdom from God, and righteousness and sanctification, (*hagiasmos*) and redemption.[31]

---

26 Salkeld, *Can Catholics and Evangelicals Agree about Purgatory and the Last Judgment?*, 42.

27 Jacques Le Goff, *The Birth of Purgatory*, trans. Arthur Goldhammer (Chicago: University of Chicago Press, 1981), 357.

28 Salkeld, *Can Catholics and Evangelicals Agree about Purgatory and the Last Judgment?*, 13–14.

29 Hebrews 10:10. See also Hebrews 9:27.

30 In the introduction of his letters, the apostle Paul refers to his Christian brethren as called saints (*klētois hagiois*). See Romans 1:7; 1 Corinthians 1:2; 2 Corinthians 1:2; Ephesians 1:2 and Colossian 1:2.

31 1 Corinthians 1:30.

At death, all believers—as sanctified ones—enter into the presence of their Lord. Who would not want to insist on gaining heaven, leading to eternal life, rather than purgatory, leading to eternal damnation!

Comparing the statistics from *Eternity before Their Eyes* with the present one concerning Christianity and Islam, the number of people who desire to go to heaven is still relatively the same. However, the most significant change between the two books is how people's belief of either cessation of existence or that they do not know what will happen to them when they die has almost reversed in a little over a decade.

Eternity before Their Eyes
(questionnaire conducted 2005–2007)

Heaven	47.5%
Cessation of existence	21.3%
I do not know	15.1%

Defending Jesus' Crucifixion
(questionnaire conducted 2015–2018)[32]

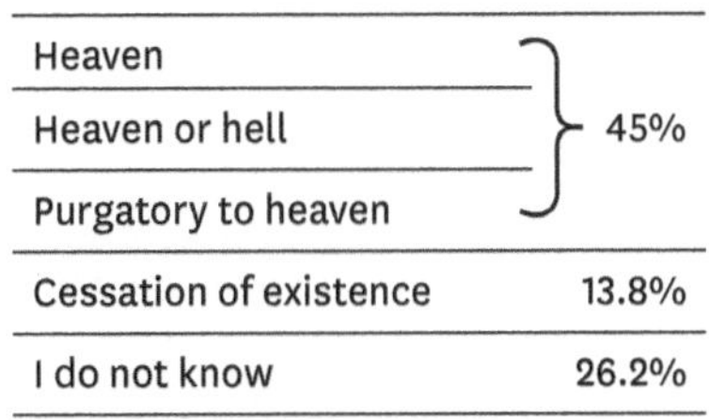

Heaven	
Heaven or hell	} 45%
Purgatory to heaven	
Cessation of existence	13.8%
I do not know	26.2%

---

32 The questionnaire was completed Saturday, January 20, 2018.

Select bibliography

Books

Afridi, Mehnaz M. *Shoah through Muslim Eyes*. Cambridge: Academic Studies Press, 2017.

al-Jabbār, 'Abd. *The Critique of Christian Origins: Qāḍī 'Abd al-Jabbār's (d. 415/1025) Islamic Essay on Christianity*, ed. trans. Gabriel Said Reynolds and Samir Khalili Samir. Provo: Brigham Young University Press, 2010.

'Ali, Maulana Muhammad. *Muhammad and Christ*. Columbus: Ahmadiyya Society for the Propogation of Islam, 1993.

'Ata ur-Rahim, Muhammad. *Jesus: Prophet of Islam*. Norfolk: Diwan Press, 1977.

'Ata ur-Rahim, Muhammad and Ahmad Thomson. *Jesus: Prophet of Islam*, rev. ed. London: Ta-Ha Publishers, 1996.

Athanasius, *Contra Gentes and De Incarnatione*. ed. and trans. by R.W. Thomson. Oxford: Clarendon Press, 1971.

Athanasius, *The Letters of Saint Athanasius concerning the Holy Spirit*, trans. C.R.B. Shapland. London: Epworth Press, 1951. https://archive.org/stream/TheLettersOfSaintAthanasiusConcerning

TheHolySpirit/Athanasius_Letters_to_Serapion_Shapland#page/
n5/mode/2up. Accessed February 21, 2020.

Ayoub, Mahmoud. *A Muslim View of Christianity: Essays on Dialogue*, ed. Irfan A. Omar. Maryknoll: Orbis, 2007.

Barnard, L.W. *Justin Martyr: His Life and Thought*. Cambridge: Cambridge University Press, 1967.

Barnes, Timothy D. *Constantine and Eusebius*. Cambridge: Harvard University Press, 1981.

Block, C. Jonn. *The Qur'an in Christian-Muslim Dialogue: Historical and Modern Interrelation*. New York: Routledge, 2013.

Bond, Helen K. *Pontius Pilate in History and Interpretation*. Cambridge: Cambridge University Press, 1998.

Brent, Allen. *Ignatius of Antioch: A Martyr Bishop and the Origin of the Episcopacy*. New York: Continuum, 2007.

Carter, Warren. *Pontius Pilate: Portraits of a Roman Governor*. Collegeville: Liturgical Press, 1989.

Casey, Maurice. *Jesus: Evidence and Argument or Mythicist Myths*. London: Bloomsburg, 2014.

Chapman, David W. and Eckhard J. Schnabel. *The Trial and Crucifixion of Jesus: Texts and Commentary*. Tübingen: Mohr Siebeck, 2015.

Chester, Stephen. "Paul and the Galatian Believers." In *The Blackwell Companion to Paul*, ed. Stephen Westerholm. Chichester: Wiley-Blackwell, 2011. 63–78.

Collins, Raymond F. *The Power of Images in Paul*. Collegeville: Liturgical Press, 2008.

Davis, Glenn, *The Development of the Canon of the New Testament* (1997–2010). http://www.ntcanon.org/Athanasius.shtml. Accessed November 17, 2016.

Drobner, Hubertus R. *The Fathers of the Church: A Comprehensive Introduction*. Trans. Siegfried Schatzmann. Peabody: Hendrickson, 2007.

Ehrman, Bart D. *Did Jesus Exist? The Historical Argument for Jesus of Nazareth*. New York: Harper Collins, 2012.

Fatoohi, Louay. *The Mystery of the Crucifixion: The Attempt to Kill Jesus in the Qur'an, the New Testament, and Historical Sources*. Birmingham: Luna Plena, 2008.

Geisler, Norman L. and Abdul Saleeb. *Answering Islam: The Crescent in Light of the Cross*. 2nd ed. Grand Rapids: Baker, 2002.

Gilchrist, John. "Origins and Sources of the Gospel of Barnabas," *Facing the Muslim Challenge: A Handbook of Christian-Muslim Apologetics* (1999). http://www.bible.ca/Islam/library/Gilchrist/barnabas/html. Accessed April 20, 2017.

Gilchrist, John. *The Qur'an and the Historical Jesus*. Benoni: Christian Resource Ministries, 2015.

The Gospel of Barnabas. Karachi: Fazleesons, 1974.

Graves, Dan, ed. "Module 109: Council of Nicea." *Christian History Institute*, (2016). https://www.christianhistoryinstitute.org/study/module/nicea/. Accessed November 15, 2016.

Green, Joel B. *The Death of Jesus: Tradition and Interpretation in the Passion Narrative*. Tübingen: J.C.B. Mohr, 1988.

Habermas, Gary R. *The Historical Jesus: Ancient Evidence for the Life of Christ*. Joplin: College Press, 2001.

Haykin, Michael A.G. *Rediscovering the Church Fathers: Who They Were and How They Shaped the Church*. Wheaton: Crossway, 2011.

Hengel, Martin. *Crucifixion: In the Ancient World and the Folly of the Message of the Cross*. Philadelphia: Fortress, 1977.

Holcomb, Justin S. *Know the Creeds and Councils*. Grand Rapids: Zondervan, 2014.

Hourihane, Colum. *Pontius Pilate, Anti-Semitism and the Passion in Medieval Art*. Princeton: Princeton University Press, 2009.

Hultgren Arland J. "Paul and the Law." In *The Blackwell Companion to Paul*, ed. Stephen Westerholm. Chichester: Wiley-Blackwell, 2011. 202–215.

"Imperial Edict Decrees Catholic Christianity—380," Christian History Institute (February 27, 2016). https://www.christianhistoryinstitute.org/dailyquote/2/27/. Accessed December 28, 2016.

Kee, Alistair. *Constantine versus Christ: The Triumph of Ideology*. London: SCM, 1982.

Kilpatrick, William. *Christianity, Islam and Atheism: The Struggle for the Soul of the West*. San Francisco: Ignatius Press, 2012.

Lawson, Todd. *The Crucifixion and the Qur'an: A Study in the History of Muslim Thought*. Oxford: Oneworld, 2009.

Leirvik, Oddbjørn. *Images of Jesus Christ in Islam*. 2nd ed. New York: Continuum, 2010.

Leithart, Peter J. *Defending Constantine: The Twilight of an Empire and the Dawn of Christendom*. Downers Grove: IVP Academic, 2010.

Macintyre, Ben. *Double Cross: The True Story of the D-Day Spies*. New York: Crown. 2012.

Macintyre, Ben. *Operation Mincement: How a Dead Man and a Bizarre Plan Fooled the Nazis and Assured an Allied Victory*. New York: Harmony, 2010.

Maqsood, Ruqaiyyah Waris. *The Mysteries of Jesus: A Muslim Study of the Origins and Doctrines of the Christian Church*. Oxford: Sakina, 2000.

Messier, Ron. *Jesus: One Man, Two Faiths—A Dialogue Between Christians and Muslims*. Raleigh: Twin Oaks, 2010.

Parrinder, G. *Jesus in the Qur'an*. London: Sheldon Press, 1965.

Pavao, Paul. "The Canons of the Council of Nicea." Christian History for Everyman (2014). http://www.christian-history.org/council-of-nicea-canons.html. Accessed November 17, 2016.

Payton Jr., James R. *Irenaeus on the Christian Faith: A Condensation of Against Heresies*. Cambridge: James Clarke, 2012.

Reynolds, Gabriel Said. *A Muslim Theologian in the Sectarian Milieu: 'Abd al-Jabbār and the Critique of Christian Origins*. Leiden: Brill, 2004.

Rusch, William G. *The Trinitarian Controversy*. Philadelphia: Fortress, 1980.

Saritoprak, Zeki. *Islam's Jesus*. Gainesville: University of Florida Press, 2014.

Schoedel, William R. *Ignatius of Antioch: A Commentary on the Letters of Ignatius of Antioch*. Philadelphia: Fortress, 1985.

Siddiqui, Mona. "Death, Resurrection and Human Destiny: Qur'anic and Islamic Perspectives." In *Death, Resurrection and Human Destiny: Christian and Muslim Perspectives*, ed. David Marshall and Lucinda Mosher. Washington: Georgetown University Press, 2014. 25–37.

Skarsaune, Oskar. "Justin and His Bible." In *Justin Martyr and His Worlds*, eds. S. Parvis and P. Foster. Minneapolis: Fortress, 2007. 77–87.

Smither, Edward L. *Rethinking Constantine: History, Theology and Legacy*. Cambridge: James Clarke, 2014.

Southern, Patricia. *The Roman Empire from Severus to Constantine*. London: Routledge, 2001.

Sox, David. *The Gospel of Barnabas*. London: George Allen and Unwin, 1984.

St. Irenaeus of Lyon. *On the Apostolic Preaching*. Trans. John Behr. Crestwood: St. Vladimir's Seminary Press, 1977.

Tanner, Norman P., ed. *Decrees of the Ecumenical Councils*. https://www.ewtn.com/catholicism/library/council-of-constance-1459. Accessed February 21, 2020.

Toland, John. *Nazarenus, or, Jewish, Gentile, and Mahometan Christianity* (1718), https://books.google.ca/books?id=PQ5PAAAAcAA-J&printsec=frontcover&source=gbs_ge_summary_r&cad=0#v=onepage&q&f=false. Accessed January 30, 2017.

Van Voorst, Robert. *Jesus Outside the New Testament*. Grand Rapids: Eerdmans, 2000.

Vermes, Géza. *Christian Beginnings: From Nazareth to Nicaea A.D. 30–325*. New York: Penguin, 2013.

Yusseff, M.A. *The Dead Sea Scrolls, The Gospel of Barnabas and the New Testament*. Indianapolis: American Trust, 1990.

Zahniser, A.H. Mathias. *The Mission and Death of Jesus in Islam and Christianity*. Maryknoll: Orbis, 2008.

Zebiri, Kate. *Muslims and Christians: Face to Face*. Oxford: Oneworld, 1997.

Articles

Ayoub, Mahmound. "Muslim Views of Christianity: Some Modern Examples." *Islamochristiana* 10 (1984): 49–70.

Joosten, Jan. "The Date and Provenance of the 'Gospel of Barnabas.'" *Journal of Theological Studies* 61 (April 2010): 200–215.

MacAdam, Henry Innis. "Quid Est Veritas? Pontius Pilate in Fact, Fiction, Film and Fantasy." *Irish Biblical Studies* 23 (April 2001): 66–99.

Notley, R. Steven. "Pontius Pilate: Sadist or Saint? *Biblical Archaeology Review* 23 (July/August 2017): 41–49, 59–60.

Pulcini, Theodore. "In the Shadow of Mount Carmel: The Collapse of the 'Latin East' and the Origins of the Gospel of Barnabas." *Islam and Christian-Muslim Relations* (April 2001): 191–209.

Retief, François Pieter and Louise Cilliers. "The history and pathology of crucifixion." *South African Medical Journal* 93 (2003): 938–941.

Reynolds, Gabriel Said. "The Rise and Fall of Qādi 'Abd al-Jabbār." *International Journal of Middle East Studies* 37 (2005): 3–18.

Slomp, Jan. "*Jesus: Prophet of Islam*: A Book Review," *The Near East School of Theology* 3 (November 1980): 35–39.

Slomp, Jan. "The 'Gospel of Barnabas' in Recent Research." *Islamochristiana* 23 (1997): 81–109.

Stern, S.M. "'Abd al-Jabbār's Account of How Christ's Religion was Falsified by the Adoption of Roman Customs." *Journal of Theological Studies* 19 (April 1968): 128–185.

Stern, S.M. "Quotations from Apocryphal Gospels in 'Abd al-Jabār." *Journal of Theological Studies* 18 (April 1967): 34–52.

Videos and documentaries

Ally, Safiyyah (host). "Gospel of Barnabas, Is it Real?—Dr. Shabir Ally," *Let the Quran Speak*. August 6, 2014. https://www.youtube.com/watch?v=KALwiuy5-5I. Accessed January 24, 2020.

Ally, Shabir. "Did Jesus Physically Rise from the Dead? An Evaluation of the Craig/Ally Debate." April 12, 2009. https://shabirally.wordpress.com/2009/04/12/did-jesus-physically-rise-from-the-dead/. Accesse February 23, 2017.

"Jesus was crucified and then rescued: Dr. Shabir Ally." September 10, 2016. https://www.youtube.com/watch?v=9L8FVuVbSSs. Accessed February 24, 2017.

"The Keys to the Reich." May 5, 2013. https://www.youtube.com/watch?v=iQOnkYVnptE&t=49s. Accessed April 29, 2017.

Macintyre, Ben. "Double Cross." December 21, 2016. https://www.youtube.com/watch?v=z8x-RGaLtgQ. Accessed April 25, 2017.

Macintyre, Ben. "Operation Mincemeat." July 2, 2015. https://www.youtube.com/watch?v=HoTXw1w7K-M. Accessed April 29, 2017.

Reeves, Ryan. "Council of Constantinople." February 23, 2015. https://www.youtube.com/watch?v=WrlR1aFODDI. Accessed December 29, 2016.

CHARLES DARWIN'S RELIGIOUS VIEWS

From creationist to
evolutionist
By David Herbert

A SPIRITUAL BIOGRAPHY that
focuses primarily on the religious experiences of Charles
Darwin's life—demonstrating
how Darwin's rejection of the
Bible led him to adopt the
naturalistic assumptions that
were foundational to his belief
in evolutionism.

ISBN 978–1-894400-30-5

CHARLES DARWIN'S RELIGIOUS JOURNEY

By David Herbert

WRITTEN FOR YOUNG PEOPLE,
this book traces Charles' life—
from his voyage around the
world on HMS *Beagle* to his
research and experiments on
his return to England. Complete with maps and photos.

ISBN 978–1-894400-34-3

COMPANION WORKBOOK
ISBN 978–1-894400-35-0

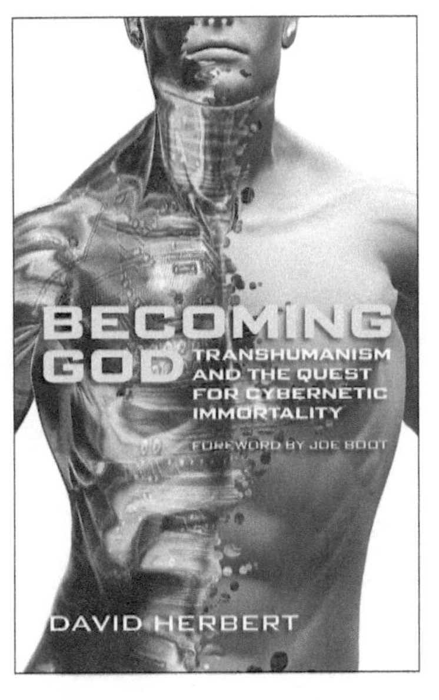

BECOMING GOD

Transhumanism and the quest for cybernetic immortality

By David Herbert

THIS BOOK TRACES the philosophic and scientific roots of the transhumanism movement —through the changes brought with The Enlightenment, the Victorian era, religious humanism and secular humanism.

Herbert profiles the movement's key world figures and reveals how changing worldviews, advancing technologies, entrenched scientific beliefs and rapidly expanding biotechnologies have led some to believe that immortality is on the horizon. Shunning death and disease, transhumanists are pursuing a future devoid of these realities and believe humankind is on the cusp of immortality—a pivotal moment they call the "Singularity."

Herbert shows how the Christian's biblical view of the body, disease and death points to a future resurrection, where believers will be given perfect, immortal bodies, once more united to their souls and spirits. The Christian's hope is not for immortality on this earth but in the new heavens and new earth.

ISBN 978-1-894400-58-9

Visit us online at www.joshuapress.com